TH PRESENT

A Practical and Spiritual Guideline to
Help You Enjoy the Ride

The Present Actor
A Practical and Spiritual Guideline to Help You Enjoy the Ride

EAN-13: 978-1477624791
ISBN-10: 1477624791
Printed in the United States of America

THIS IS ONE HUMONGOUS DEDICATION

There are many people whose presence, insight and/or support has brought me to the place of writing this book.

I owe particular thanks to the women who put me on this specific road – I've been fortunate to work for some of the smartest in the business. The late Iris Burton always said that I should be a casting director and set the wheels in motion. My good friend, the one and only Alexa Fogel, jumped through hoops to get me hired as her casting assistant and has always made me feel more intelligent than I am just by knowing her. Donna Rosenstein decided to take a chance on an annoyingly optimistic assistant and promoted me to casting director. Much gratitude also goes to Keli Lee, who so generously took me under her wing so many years ago.

Of course a ton of love goes to my wonderful husband Louis, who always grows along with me and never gets pissed when I have to work until 11pm! Having a Great Guy (as well as a funny guy) is a huge gift that I never take for granted.

I'm grateful to my best friends Geoff Soffer (my gay soul-mate), John Ort (the biggest heart I know), Kirsten Ames (my eternal gal pal), dearest chum Janet Murphy, the much beloved Rosalie Joseph, Honey Bear Chuck Bunting, my brilliant buddy Sandi Logan, the incredibly luminous Harry Ford and my personal hero Ray Fisher, who all give me immeasurable support and love!

I'm thankful to my Family – Freckles of love to Dad's positive spirit and to Mom, "with every fiber of my being". I thank my talented, wonderful brother Stephen for always being there to make me laugh and for bringing my dear sister-in-law Kathia and beautiful whoopee-pie niece Aria into my life. I'm lucky to have married into a family of such kind in-laws, especially my great sister-in-law Sue Davis.

Dr. Wayne Dyer and Dan Millman have my infinite gratitude for showing me The Way with everything they've written.

Sam Christensen, Jamie Forster, Shane Hoffman and Ken Klein have all played a significant role in my arrival to this particular place.

Years of appreciation go to all of my past and present co-worker buddies – especially the ones who've been in the trenches with me for so many years: my fantastic boss and friend Ayo Davis, Claudia Ramsumair, John Villacorta and Brian Dorfman. My uber-talented NY team members Erica Hart, Laura Janeczko and Blaine Johnston are my second family – the love, creativity and fun that we share every day is invaluable. Many thanks to all of the fantastic casting directors, agents and managers who help to make my job so rewarding! The world is a better place because of my dear friends/ favorite acting coaches: the inestimable guru-to-all Bob Krakower and Ted Sluberski, probably the smartest and wittiest guy I know.

Of course this book wouldn't be possible without all of the fantastic actors out there that have given me much more than I could ever hope to give back to them.

People show up in your life for various reasons, but ultimately everyone is there to teach you something.....so I thank everyone!

DISCLAIMER

The opinions expressed in this book are solely those of the author and do not represent the views of ABC Entertainment, The Walt Disney Company or any of its subsidiaries. Furthermore, ABC Entertainment, The Walt Disney Company and any of its subsidiaries assume no responsibility or liability for the content of this book.

All health-related information presented within this book is informational only and should not be considered as a substitute for consultation with a duly-licensed medical doctor. Any attempt to diagnose or treat an illness, minor or major, should come under the direction of a physician or other licensed health care provider. The author is not a medical doctor and does not purport to offer medical advice, make diagnoses or prescribe remedies for specific conditions. Reliance on any health information in this book is solely at your own risk.

The author assumes no liability or responsibility for any damage or injury that may occur in any capacity from the use or interpretation of any information in this book.

At this point you must be wondering "what the Hell is in this book, anyway??!"

TABLE OF CONTENTS

CHAPTER 6

ABOUT THE AUTHOR

So Who Am I To Judge?

There's no such thing as Absolute Truth. An impressionable person may read a book like this and accept every word as law. A cynical person or someone with a different life experience may reject it altogether. I think the truth lies somewhere in between the two...absorb what makes sense to you and leave the rest behind. You should seriously consider guidance from people you respect but be aware that many different roads can lead you to wherever it is that you're going.

As actors, most of you put a lot of weight on what a casting director says and what they think of you. Obviously, to get the job you usually need to get past the casting director first - but we aren't magical, all-knowing beings - we're just people. A casting director can be someone who is highly knowledgeable about actors and their craft or simply a subjective person with an opinion. The majority of casting directors are extremely smart and capable but, as with every other profession, there's no One Truth. So in case you're curious, here are a few paragraphs about who I am...read it or skip it altogether, it's simply here for those of you that would like a reference point!

I'm happy to say that I was literally born into this business - right between the matinee and evening performances of "Damn Yankees". My Dad was a Broadway comedian/ dancer/singer and was in the original production of many other classic musicals, such as "Guys and Dolls" and "A Funny Thing Happened on the Way to the Forum". When I was past my infancy, he immediately started teaching me how to read so he would always have someone to do his sides with him....so it's no exaggeration to say that I've been doing this close to my entire life! We'd spend countless hours watching old movies together and my Dad would point out great acting moments from Charles Laughton, Spencer Tracey, Jimmy Stewart, et al. My Mom was an accomplished Broadway and Ed Sullivan dancer, so most of my childhood memories are of growing up backstage and around actors. I was fortunate to have a very colorful childhood - from watching the Chorus Girls put in their falsies to sitting on both Zero Mostel and Judy Garland's laps to seeing Broadway stars lying naked in the dressing rooms getting "shots" in their butt by "doctors". I wouldn't trade those memories for anything, but there were many difficult times as well. I saw my Dad lose acting jobs that were a sure thing and life was generally a crazy, unstable ride of Feast or Famine. My Dad's disappointment and uncertainty therefore became my own and I had to learn how to deal with it from a very, very early age. One thing, however, was certain - when that call came in from a casting director with an audition or a job, it was always an incredibly happy day....so I have always equated That Call with Happiness.

I've lived many lives within this one so far - I was a child actress briefly and got my Equity card at age 10 when the course of my life was thrown in another direction...but that's a whole other story for a whole other book! When I became an adult, I married an actor (what else?), moved to LA....and 14 years later divorced said actor.....but he's a very private person so I won't go into that either. Suffice it to say that I moved back to NY and it was time to explore what I really wanted. For a while I was certain that I would be a Holistic Healer, as Alternative Medicine and all things New

Age-y and Spiritual fascinate me as much as the world of acting. However, I quickly came to the conclusion that advice for healing suits me better as a happy amateur! So it was a no-brainer for me to simply pursue what I had been doing all of my life anyway -- lovingly observing, critiquing, adjusting, analyzing and simply being there for actors.

Although there are now courses in a few schools for this profession, everyone comes to casting from a different road. I cast a few off-off Broadway shows, a film that went to Sundance and secured an internship at the NY ABC casting office. I worked very hard, feeling blessed and happy every day just to be there. I'm now the head of that office and if you read my Dedication, you'll see that there are really wonderful people in this business who helped (and continue to help) me along the way.

Being a casting director is so much more than a way to make a living or simply "something I can do". I was in love with everything about this job from the start and if I won the Lottery tomorrow, I would be back at work the next day.

I'm married to a wonderful actor that I've been with for many years, and over 90% of my friends are actors. In a way, things have come full circle from when I was a kid -- now I get to make that wonderful call that will make someone happy! I believe that we all have our unique mission in life, and I have definitely found mine.

INTRODUCTION

What Do I Mean By "The Present Actor"?

There are two meanings to this title - one is rather straightforward and pragmatic, the other is more metaphysical.

The "Pragmatic":

The ability to Be Present is something that every great actor has in common. The Present Actor is one who is emotionally and physically connected to his or her circumstance. I know, this is very simplistic Acting 101 stuff, but spend one day with me in a casting session and see how many actors forget this basic precept! If you have any hope of suspending the disbelief of your audience and engaging them in what you're doing, then Being Present is crucial. If your third eye is out there watching and judging your every move, it's going to be extremely difficult to experience and convey anything resembling Truth. Many actors get too caught up in pleasing whoever is watching them to give an audition or performance that ends up meaning anything at all. Too much pandering can lead to inauthentic choices and stifled instincts. If you don't entirely believe what you're doing, then we won't either! From the simplicity of James Cagney's "Learn your lines, find your mark, look 'em in the eye and tell 'em the truth." to the more detailed Meisner technique, there are many, many different philosophies about how to achieve this kind of honesty and focus. There is no "right way" or "wrong way" there is just the way that works for you.

The "Metaphysical":

I'm not going into any details here about the fourteen year chapter of my life that was spent in LA. Suffice it to say that I was friends with or around many, many A-List movie stars, producers and directors for all those years and have numerous stories regarding these adventures (that's a whole other book that I'll never write!). These celebrities may very well be talented, brilliant and special in varying degrees... but the bottom line is that they are just people with the same bodily functions, kind or empty hearts and emotional baggage as your mail carrier, dentist or accountant. The most valuable thing that I observed in those years was that the people who were unhappy and fearful before they became successful were inevitably still unhappy and fearful after they became successful. Once the initial glittering confetti of "woo-hoo, I'm accepted, rich and famous!" had settled down to earth, they were ultimately left with their same old self. Because they had mistakenly identified the answer to their problems as something external, they assumed that once they achieved that external prize that they would be happy. Wrong! This realization added a touch of desperation to their unhappy/fearful cocktail, because now there was nothing left outside of themselves to blame for their negative emotional state. Fame doesn't magically change who you are internally, it just intensifies it. As you can guess, the people who were basically happy and loving life before they became successful were still happy and loving life (even more so!) after they became successful. The lesson here is that you can't put your life on hold, thinking that you won't truly be happy until some unpredictable, external circumstance happens. All we have is today, but most of us find it very difficult to Be Present and appreciate this moment. We're constantly planning, plotting and scheduling for tomorrow - but is that really the most fulfilling way to live? I don't think you can afford to live in an illusion of the future and disregard all of the beautiful things that you actually do have right now.

Whatever your issues are, they're going to drag along with you no matter how high you go. So work on yourself now. Work on becoming a more grateful, compassionate and peaceful person - because all anyone truly has with any certainty is today.

What lies behind us and what lies before us are small matters compared to what lies within us.
- Ralph Waldo Emerson

CHAPTER I

YOU ARE EXACTLY WHERE YOU'RE SUPPOSED TO BE.

It's pretty simple - if you were meant to be anywhere else, you would be there. This applies to everyone, but it's especially relevant to those of you that are struggling along the path to "success". You're running around (literally and figuratively), trying to figure out why you haven't been seen by this casting director or tested for that pilot or landed the role that will bring you to the next level. The answer is very simple. You're not ready. Please don't misunderstand me - by "ready" I'm not necessarily talking about your talent. You could be the most brilliant actor on the face of this Earth and yet not be ready emotionally. You may not be ready spiritually. There may be some things that you still need to experience and learn before you get what you think you should have already achieved. The universe has a way of giving you exactly what you need when you need it. Unfortunately, this doesn't always correspond with what you *want*, but time has a way of proving that you are not always the best judge of what should or shouldn't be in your life at this particular moment. Take love relationships, for example. It's a pretty safe bet that you have at least one relationship in your past that didn't turn out the way you had envisioned it would. At the time, emotional creature that you are, it made you absolutely miserable to be without that person. He or she was The One, there will never be anyone else for you, etc., etc. Well, time goes by and eventually you meet a fantastic person that makes you really happy.

When you think back to your ex, you thank the stars above that you're no longer with that other person. You see now why he or she was not ultimately right for you, although you couldn't (or didn't want to) see it at the time. All of the things you learned from that previous relationship paved the way for this one to come into your life.

This applies to your career desires as well. You may want something very badly (love in the case of relationships, a certain standard of success in the case of your career), but trust that if it's not happening, it's because it's not right for this particular time and place for you. There are still more lessons to be learned before you get what you thought you were so ready for yesterday. Think back to who you were just three years ago – you've learned a lot in these three years and grown in numerous ways. Because of this, there are situations and events that you're only now truly ready for. It's also possible that what you thought you wanted back then isn't even what ends up making you the happiest of all.

Give It Up -- Or Stay?

You're devoting your life to a calling that's enmeshed in a business that seemingly has no logic. Eeek! Acting is one of the few professions that promises absolutely nothing. If you were a talented and gifted doctor, lawyer, mechanic or plumber, you would get the proper education and then logically expect to make some sort of decent living in your field. But acting? Well, even a great actor can find him-or-herself unemployed more often than they had ever thought possible.

This is where perseverance comes in. Some truly fine actors have given it up because they've had the passion kicked right out of them. I understand that - many actors are by definition more sensitive than the next person - but it's that very sensitivity that makes it impossible for some to have the tough skin necessary to go on.

That's why people often advise you to go into another profession if there's anything else that could possibly make you happy. I actually admire the ones that leave acting and find happiness elsewhere as much as I applaud the ones that could never even imagine doing anything else and stick it out no matter what. It takes courage to leave and it takes courage to stay.

Then there are some of you that are simply destined for another path. Your original dream of being an actor might be tweaked into something you will ultimately find even more exciting. Many directors, producers, screenwriters, playwrights, teachers, casting directors, agents and managers are ex-actors. Creative fulfillment comes in many forms and your true calling may simply be untapped.

But being an actor can be as much a part of you as your blood type and just as undeniable. If you're in it for the long haul, be prepared for exactly that. Even if you've enjoyed success, everything is cyclical and what goes up must come down....the question is, do you have the perseverance to wait for the next upswing?

"Perseverance is a great element of success. If you knock long enough and loud enough at the gate, you are sure to wake up somebody."
- Henry Wadsworth Longfellow

You Are Here

A countless number of Name Actors have told me that, in hindsight, they probably wouldn't have been ready for success if it had happened any earlier for them. It's a rare occurrence when I meet an actor who doesn't believe that he or she is ready to be a star now. But as I said earlier, think of yourself a few years ago – you may very well have had the same thought then too, but haven't you grown in a myriad of ways since then? Everything that happens to you in your day-to-day existence...the great stuff, the crap...it's all contributing to your growth as a person and as an artist. Why would you want to put yourself out there in front of millions and millions of people in an embryonic state? The entertainment business is littered with examples of one-hit-wonders and people who were thrust into the spotlight too soon, and very few of them survive it well.

> *"It does not matter how slowly you go so long as you do not stop."*
> *- Confucius*

When you look at a large map in a Mall, there is always an arrow or large red circle that states You Are Here. This is so you can get your bearings and figure out the path that will take you wherever it is you want to go. In order to reach your destination, it's important to honestly see Where You Are now in relation to that goal. It can take a lot of soul-searching to be clear and honest about where you are. Sometimes it's difficult to look at this because you may have to admit that you're farther away from your goals than you'd like to be. But you're not running a race here, so take a breath if you need to, deconstruct if you have to. Self-evaluate in order to determine the steps that will move you towards your objective. At this point you'll have a clearer vision about the steps you need to take to ultimately show up to the party at your strongest. Sometimes this can even mean temporarily taking yourself out of the game. I really, really admire the actor that knows him or herself well enough to do this. I have a good friend who was doing very well in this business - he had a Series Regular role in a pilot as well as one of the most coveted agents and managers in the business. In the midst of all of this, he decided to go to Grad School because he just knew that the experience would greatly benefit him. For the same reason, an actor might put her/himself in class or a private study situation because they want to feel 100% confident in what they're doing. This isn't just for those who are new to the business or chronically under-employed. There are many very accomplished actors I know who realize that they may not be operating at their full potential. To have that kind of self-awareness and the clarity to do something about it is truly a beautiful thing! Anything less is simply the Ego talking, so stop pressuring yourself with the false notion that you should know all the answers. It's the wise person who understands that there's always more to learn.

The Futility Of Blame

Obtaining anything resembling true happiness as an actor may very well come down to how honest you are with yourself. If your career isn't progressing the way you expected it to, there's usually a reason beyond "this business sucks!" The nature of this business is totally beside the point. You give away every ounce of power that you have over your life when you point your finger at *anything* outside of yourself as the cause for your predicament. Sure, in the short term it may be very comforting and even gratifying to stay on the Treadmill of Blame -- railing against how "they" (or life) won't give you a break. But do you really want to live a powerless life filled with resentment and/or jealousy? This very destructive and negative state of mind is manufactured entirely by you and you alone. Do you doubt that? If so, I think it's a safe bet that you aren't happy with your life at the moment. It's time to put down that defensive armor - it's heavy, it's exhausting and it's weighing you down. If you want power over your life, you must take a good amount of responsibility for everything that happens to you. Blame is a distraction from the work on yourself you need to be focusing on, that will actually make a huge difference in your life. Has blame ever really helped you? Sure, I can understand how some momentary comfort can be gotten by putting the way your career and/or life is going on the shoulders of external events and other people - but it's ultimately just self-deception. If you want to be sucked into the black hole of *that* abyss, then you've simply chosen to live the rest of your life in a self-fulfilling prophesy.

Here is an example of how playing the blame game can become an endless hamster wheel of excuses as to "Why my career isn't where I want it to be":

"It's because I don't have an agent"....*and then you get an agent.*

But then...

"It's because my agent never calls me"...*and then your agent calls you.*

But then...

"It's because my agent only calls me with small roles"... *and then your agent gets you in for a large role.*

But then...

"It's because the casting directors never bring me in for producers"...*and then the casting director brings you in for the producers*

But then...

"It's because the producers are always 'going another way' with the role"

...and you can see how this can go on and on if you're never content with your progress and always attributing your discontent to others....

If you make it through this, does it stop once you become "successful"? Not if you're still living in that head of yours! Success doesn't change you. Success only intensifies who you already are. So now the reason you're not happy becomes:

"It's because my agent is a bonehead"

"It's because my director is an idiot"

"It's because my co-star is a jerk"

"It's because (fill-in-the-name-of-rising-star) is getting my roles"

...and you wonder why you're "successful" but not happy? It's not you against the world - YOU create your world, so that makes it you against yourself. It's a strange phenomenon that what you think about usually has a way of manifesting itself. Focus on disappointment, rejection and defeat and that's probably what you'll get... Be grateful for all of the wonderful things that you DO have instead of fixating on whatever it is that you DON'T have. When you think someone's a schmuck, challenge that response and try to see them as someone who's simply trying to do their best with whatever limited tools they have. Just like you.

Take a deep look inside and try being the person that you would want to be in a foxhole with! You can't change everyone else, so make a change for the better in yourself. Just for fun. Let's see what happens.

> *It is better to light one candle*
> *than to curse the darkness.*
> *- Chinese Proverb*

This Business Is Friggin' Hard...So What Should You Do?

Many of us are continuously looking to have some modicum of control over our lives, and one way that we think we can achieve that is through having a strategy or "plan of attack". I've heard countless actors over the years devise their One, Three or Five Year Plan: "Within one year, I will have an agent" "Within two years, I will be on a TV Series, in a Major Film, etc." I applaud the determination and optimism of this kind of thinking, but we're in the Entertainment Business. I'm into The Secret as much as anybody, but there's no way that everything is going to happen exactly the way you want it to. That means that every dream may or may not come true despite your talent or lack thereof, despite your looks or lack thereof, despite your prestigious Grad School Degree or lack thereof. The only thing I can safely say is that if you're unanimously regarded as both brilliant and gorgeous, you have a better chance than most at getting what you want from this business. This is by no means a guarantee that you'll live happily ever after, but you'll probably have a successful career. Other than that scenario, there's very little logic involved. Yes, a plan can be a great motivator to get you out of bed in the morning - all I ask is that you not be devastated if said plan falls apart. That won't be so frightening if you see it as the universe simply making way for a new path. Events rarely happen in a predictable way and, if you can't change them, you must be willing to flow with whatever happens. While you're at it, go a step further and trust in the notion that everything happens the way it's supposed to. Maybe this turn of events wasn't your choice, but it might be steering you away from something really unpleasant that you just can't see from here. This road might even take you to an amazing place if you'll simply allow it to. A disappointing event can be a great teacher - attempt to understand the significance of this particular lesson and grow from it.

So now that I've more or less crapped on the concept that having "A Plan" is necessarily the answer, what should you do?

Well, there are universal truths and yet everyone is unique in their approach to - and denial of - success...

Ask yourself what you haven't been willing to do to achieve your goal:

Are you working on your craft every day? There are a myriad of things you can do to become a better, richer actor...Take a great class, watch classic performances in movies, go and see whatever theater you can afford, write your own screenplay, get together with your actor friends and film sketches for the internet, film your own webisodes, put up or simply read plays together, etc. etc. etc. Just the act of doing, watching or listening to anything that truly inspires you emotionally, spiritually or creatively will undoubtedly help you along your path.

Are you devoting the amount of time that you should to your auditions (much more on that in Chapter 2 - The Art of Auditioning!)?

Are you letting your fears stop you? If you live in Iowa, are you afraid to make the move to New York? If you live in New York, are you afraid to leave your comfort zone to see what L.A. might be like? If you are unhappy living in LA, are you afraid to take your chances in New York? You may have dreams of being a big fish in a big pond -- but many people find their bliss being a big fish in a small pond. Hell, there's more to being an actor in this country than NY and LA - are you afraid to admit that maybe your happiness lies in Chicago, Boston or in Regional Theater, USA? If you've already achieved a certain level of success, are you afraid to totally own and embrace that? Are you afraid that it will go away? If you haven't reached anything near your potential, are you not permitting yourself to want more because you're afraid that it won't happen?

Are you allowing anything or anyone to make you doubt yourself?

I could go on and on, but the bottom line is – as an actor, you are your own work of art. You are creating something totally unique (you), so you have to listen to *your* gut. You are a perpetual work in progress, and that in itself should be - and is - the joy. If acting jobs aren't coming your way, *work on yourself*. If you have success but find that you're still not happy, *work on yourself*. You don't need me to tell you the areas in which you need to improve yourself – you know what they are. If that means going to the gym, the shrink, a scene study class, your house of worship, all or none of the above – you know. Maybe you've been focusing <u>*too much*</u> on yourself and need to experience the joys and epiphanies that helping someone else can bring to your life. Start with the people around you – isn't there someone that could use a sympathetic ear or a kind gesture? You may need to step outside of your usual experience for the clarity and perspective that volunteering in a homeless shelter or hospital ward will bring you. Get out of your head and look around - everyone has a story and everyone could benefit from a good word, deed or thought. Or maybe you simply need to step away from this circus for a while so you can just take a long, deep breath.

> **"Men are anxious to improve their circumstances, but are unwilling to improve themselves."**
>
> *- James Allen*

Stop disempowering yourself and become a more centered, focused person. When you're on the right path, everything in your life seems to fall into place. It's truly "The Law of Attraction" at work – positive energy out brings you positive energy back. Try to see every "lack" in your career and life as a lesson that's presented to you in this moment. Make a conscious effort to learn from it all and you'll find yourself moving forward with a lot less effort.

The Endless Abyss Of Negativity

No one I know is an Enlightened Zen Master, so let's just accept that there will be times that we find ourselves feeling a bit of self-pity. Hey, we're all human, and an undeniable part of being human is having negative feelings and experiences.

We all get fearful, angry and defensive... I'm not saying to deny that. What I am saying is to experience your negative reaction and then do everything in your power to let it go. Find any way you can, no matter how small, to make yourself feel better. No, no, no - NOT alcohol, drugs or any other self-destructive behavior that may be a quick fix now but will inevitably and viciously bite you in the ass. Although you may say "it makes me feel better", the whole point is to go from a negative energy to a positive energy and I'm pretty certain that "self-destructive" isn't synonymous with "positive"!

Sooner or later you'll have to stop looking outside of yourself for answers because they're simply never there. Come on, how many times did you see "The Wizard of Oz" as a kid - were you not paying attention?!

> *"...if I ever go looking for my heart's desire again, I won't look any further than my own back yard....because if it isn't there, I never really lost it to begin with."*
> *- Judy Garland as Dorothy*

You may roll your eyes, but this is a classic story for a reason. The journey towards some semblance of self-enlightenment is the one true universal story, as the late, great Joseph Campbell's quintessential book "The Hero with a Thousand Faces" illustrates. Both "Star Wars" and "The Matrix" used Campbell's book as one of the inspirations for their screenplays, and those films were huge hits for bigger reasons than their special effects. Your path in life is the ultimate thrill-ride, filled with wonder and unexpected twists and turns. But we could never appreciate what is great, exciting and beautiful without having the contrast and understanding that the occasional crap and chaos in life can give us. Notice I said *occasional!* If you find yourself constantly in negative situations, that's not what life is throwing at you - that's the mindset that *you* are throwing at life. That sounds like a self-help cliché because it is -- but it's also very true.

As I said earlier, you are the creator of your universe and everything exists as you perceive it. If you think the world is a cruel, rotten place or if you think the world is an adventurous, beautiful place -- you're right either way.

Don't think for one second that you aren't playing a huge part in creating what comes into your life -- everything from the things you want to the things that you don't. If your attitude is that life is unfair and you're probably never going to make it in this business, then the Universe catches that energy and pitches it right back to you... a bunch of unfair events happen and you continue not to make it in this business. You may counter to me that you started out with great optimism but the business beat you down and made you this way. I say, if this is truly your calling, if this is what you love to do beyond all else, then nothing and no one can beat you down except -- you got it -- yourself. Because stumbling blocks will always be a fact of life in this business and the sooner you learn how to finesse and circumvent them, the better. There's a proverb that some guy in the Fortune Cookie factory made up that says "You can't stop the waves, but you can learn to surf"...

Nothing can bring you peace but yourself.
- Ralph Waldo Emerson

Every bit of negative energy, from having bitter thoughts about something to screaming at the top of your lungs at someone, invites every frustrating thing that you don't want into your life. Take a moment and really think about what you're putting out there!

There are many disguises that negativity can wear, so don't fool yourself. Any time you feel jealousy for someone else's success, you are impeding your own. Some of you may look at another actor that you deem less talented than you and grumble about why they've "made it" and you haven't. And that right there is a missing piece of the puzzle - one of those things that you may need to learn before going forward. Be very careful not to look at others and measure your success (or lack of it) according to theirs. Someone else's good fortune doesn't diminish your own. Someone else's failure will never boost your potential success. Your road is a very distinct and unique one. No one else could walk in your shoes or have exactly what you have, and vice-versa. You know this innately already. Put it into practice. I firmly believe that if it's meant to be your job, nothing and no one (other than yourself) can take it away from you. So why not loosen your grip, open your heart and just be happy for your peers instead of seeing them as competition?

A candle loses nothing by
lighting another candle.
- Erin Majors

Even looking over the fence to see what auditions your friends and acquaintances are getting can be tricky if it's not done for the right reason. The right reason would be to simply know what's going on within the landscape -- the wrong reason is to confirm your fears and fuel your dissatisfaction. What forward movement can be achieved by knowing that someone else has more auditions than you do? You aren't them and they aren't you. Is that a news flash? You may think that you should be up for all the same roles as a particular person, but you may also be sorely mistaken. You may read a Breakdown (I won't tell) and think "This is me! This is my life story!", but there are hundreds of other actors who are feeling the same way, at the same time, about this same role....maybe 2% of which are actually correct in that assessment. I'm not saying that you aren't in that 2% - maybe you are. But it's that desperate feeling of "I'm missing out, I have to do something to make sure that I'm not missing out" that can be debilitating. There's a subtle undercurrent of panic here that is not only an unhealthy state for your body to be in, but an unnecessary one as well. I say unnecessary because you are creating it all. You are creating the need to be "there" - the need to be there by a certain time - to be there in a specific way - and you've convinced yourself that you won't be happy until that's fulfilled. So you have become your own jailer. Give yourself the biggest gift that anyone could ever give themselves. Give yourself the permission to trust that the universe will give you what you need when you need it. Know that when you open your heart and view everything in your life with compassion, a sense of humor and love, that's precisely what the universe will show you as well.

The way is not in the sky.
The way is in the heart.

- Buddha

CHAPTER 2:

THE ART OF AUDITIONING

When it's going good, it's amazing - but there are many times when being an actor can be extremely frustrating (No?! Really?!). There are very few professions where training and skill guarantee absolutely nothing. You can never assume anything - least of all that "your talent will speak for itself." So how in the world does a trained or simply-born-talented actor get to the next level? Although there are definitely no hard and fast rules, there are many constants in this business that would be extremely helpful for any actor to know. Probably the most important component is understanding - and I mean truly understanding - how to audition.

My biggest surprise when I became a casting director was discovering that an enormous number of actors don't audition well. Even some that I already knew as very talented seemed pedestrian and uninteresting in their auditions. It soon became clear as to why -- no one ever tells you HOW MUCH we expect. Maybe you took an Audition Class with someone who presented themselves as an "expert", but if they've never been a casting director in the medium that you're auditioning for -- I would be careful. Take the time to vet whomever you are allowing to instruct you! I've heard way too many outrageous "rules" that actors have told me were given to them in an Audition Class. A big one is "don't memorize the dialogue - it makes you seem arrogant and that your performance is now set and undirectable". Wow - that's just ridiculous. There are differing views as to how much memorization will or won't help you in an audition for theater, but no relatively sane person is going to think that you're arrogant because you were prepared and professional. Okay, insert joke here regarding "no relatively sane person"! As for on-camera auditions, I'll gladly carve it in stone that you're at a huge disadvantage if you don't try to memorize the dialogue – but more on that later. Also understand that you are the final judge as to what you choose to accept into your consciousness as Truth. Take anything that anyone says - myself included - and absorb what rings true for you and discard what doesn't. No one - and I mean no one - is such an expert that you should ignore your gut instincts in deference to them. But understand that you have to be honestly in touch with those instincts if you're going to use them as your sole guide!

Please understand that very little in life is true 100% of the time and for every "Rule" there's probably an example of someone who successfully broke it. What I'm talking about here is what I've found to be true 95% of the time.

So here are some of the constants that I have learned over the decades. Maybe you've discovered most of them already....maybe there are a few that you haven't:

Why Did My Character Say "Hi" Instead Of "Hello"?

You can never over-prepare, but you can definitely over-think. I could have written that sentence five times in a row because it's so misunderstood and ultimately so important. Thorough preparation is crucial for every actor except the .01% who have the rare gift of being captivating when reading a grocery list out loud. Preparation in short means strong opinions and choices for everything you're doing and saying, memorization, understanding how to put your unique spin on it and keeping it honest. Over-thinking is being overly concerned with the minutia of the character's background, making up irrelevant details about the character's relationships and attributing complex meanings to things where none is warranted. Over-thinking can simply be putting too much emphasis and energy into details of no consequence and running it into the ground because you're not trusting yourself. But, hey - if you're booking lots of jobs through this method, don't listen to me! If it ain't broke, don't fix it - but if you recognize yourself as someone who over-thinks your auditions, I think the odds are good that something there can use a little fixing!

Theater, Series Regulars, Under 5's, Film, Commercials – Not The Same!

Know what medium you're auditioning for. There are some actors out there who are simply so genuine and brilliant with their craft that they can give the same style of audition no matter what arm of the business it's for. They always instinctually bring interesting, unique and intelligent choices to everything they do, always know how much is too much, how little is too little, and simply don't have a dishonest acting bone in their body. These actors are in the minority and we don't come across them often. The majority of actors need at least some amount of guidance - and this means everyone from the incredibly gifted and special actors to the ones who should probably be thinking about another profession. Obviously, the Entertainment Business is made up of quite a few different vehicles for an actor to participate in - Film, Theater, Television, New Media, Commercials, Voiceovers, etc. From what I've seen, not all of you have taken into consideration that an audition that works for one medium doesn't necessarily work for another. For example, auditioning for a Series Regular or a recurring role on television can be very different than auditioning for other mediums. Think about it. When you audition for theater, the play is already written. When you audition for a film, the screenplay is already written. When you audition for a Day Player, Co-Star or Guest

Star on a television show, the episode is already written. What is required of the character and what we need is there on the page. This character will likely never be seen or heard from again (discounting sequels to films or the few times that a one-time Guest Star becomes a recurring role or Series Regular), so the producers have a more finite idea about what they'll need from you. In contrast, a television pilot is more of a blueprint....there's a "bible" that the writers have presented as an outline for many episodes ahead, but where these characters will end up 3 or 5 years from now hasn't been determined. The same goes for a new series regular role on an existing TV show. The producers, studio and network are looking at you and discerning what shape this character will take through your personality. We need to see what you'll bring to the table that the other contenders won't. That's why it's so important for us to see your unique self in the audition - it's what the writers will be drawing from in the ongoing creation of your role. Don't get me wrong - I'm not saying that every trait a character has on a series necessarily belongs to the actor playing him or her. There may be many roles out there that will have a different political view, temperament or sexual orientation than yours. If this is the case, we still want to see YOU within this person that simply has an alternate perception or way of living. Many actors don't get this. If the character is an obsessive Type A personality and you're a free spirit, you're probably not going to go in and change that concept – but hopefully you are going to give them a very distinctive Type A from your unique vantage point. So no - not every personality trait of the character is taken from the actor's life, but you are certainly a fun and invaluable well to draw from. If you're a Sports fanatic, down the line your character may very well end up being a Fantasy Football nut. The writers want to be excited about writing for you, and this can only be discerned through the imaginative and unique choices that you come in with. Therefore it's important that we get a sense of who you are and what kind of goodies you'll bring to the series from what you do in your audition. If you're questioning how to do that, see "We Want To Love You" in this chapter!

Where's The Camera?

You already know not to upstage yourself in theater – well, the same principle holds true for on-camera as well. We need to see your face, not your profile or the back of your head! Just know where the camera is so you can cheat towards it. If the reader is to the left of the camera and there are other people you're talking to in the scene, place the other characters equidistant to the right of the camera so we get a good look at your adorable face! And don't worry about remembering which side of the camera you had placed "Bob" on if there are multiple people in the scene, because we probably don't remember either!

Don't look into the camera unless you know that they want you to purposely break the fourth wall (films such as "Ferris Bueller", TV shows such as "The Office", "Modern Family" or anytime you're playing an on-air journalist). Even then, it doesn't hurt to ask the casting director if it's OK for you to use the camera.

And Here's A Samurai Sword

I like props in an audition, but ay yi yi this is such a subjective topic that you'll no doubt get differing opinions. Whatever people normally carry around with them is usually regarded as acceptable. A cellphone, iPod, blackberry, bottle of water, briefcase, bag, magazine, pad, pen, jacket, etc. are all fair game. On the other hand, a baseball bat just gives the impression of trying a little too hard! Don't let props steal the focus from you. We'd rather see the imagination in your acting choices than your prop choices, but sometimes a fun prop can work for you. Whatever you choose, just make sure that the prop doesn't outshine or hinder you in any way. If you're eating in a scene and you choose to bring actual food into your audition, make sure that you've given this a few trial runs at home first. Food may not get swallowed in time for your dialogue, it may get stuck in your teeth, etc. etc. – so be prepared! You can easily mime certain things instead - but for the most part, please keep it subtle and only when necessary. Miming is tricky and is determined on a case-by-case basis. At any rate, don't put your energy in the wrong place - it's your acting choices, not your prop choices, that we're ultimately interested in seeing.

Remember What Mom Told You

Don't slump forward if you're seated in an on-camera audition, resting your forearms on your thighs. This may be a comfortable way to sit but it diminishes your power onscreen because your shoulders are now hunched over and your whole upper body is angled downwards. Sitting up or back in the chair, even all the way back makes you look better because your face is more in line with the camera and your shoulders are filling the frame. This doesn't mean that you can never lean forward for an intimate moment or to make a point - just don't stay there!

We Want You To Be Comfortable

Don't be afraid to ask for what you need. If you walk into an audition and a chair is there but you really want to stand (or vice-versa), ask us. If you want the reader to pause somewhere because you have something planned for that pause, ask us. If you don't understand something in the scene and you can't make up a logical explanation in your head, ask us. If you don't know the pronunciation of a word or term, ask us. We may or may not be able to help you, but we'll at least try. If you aren't clear on something, chances are that other actors had or will have the exact same question. Don't feel that you'll be perceived as high maintenance or unintelligent for asking a question. Knowing the answer will make you feel more comfortable in the audition and therefore more confident in what you're doing. I believe that it's the casting director's job to make this process as comfortable for you as possible.

No Staring Contests, Please

This is more for you Newbies out there, but don't keep your eyes locked like a homing device on the reader throughout the entire scene. The only time in life that we do anything remotely like this is when we're madly in love for the first few months - then the rest of the world starts filtering back in! Okay, also maybe if you're playing a person that's insane or menacing that's staring someone down – but for the entire scene? Schmacting! No one commands 100% of our attention 100% of the time and nothing screams "I'm an actor doing a scene" louder than this. There are many moments in a conversation when you're essentially talking/thinking out loud to yourself and the other person is simply there as a witness. There are many moments that you look to the other person for affirmation. Then there are those moments when you really need something concrete from this person in front of you. We are always, to some degree, mentally multitasking in life and so it shall be in your audition!

We Want To Love You!

Although I've cast for Film and Theater in the past, the majority of my life is about casting Series Regulars on TV. When it comes to Series Regular auditions, we need to know you better after your audition than we did before your audition. What exactly does that mean? Ask your friends to list a couple of things about you that makes them want to have you in their life. Don't ask your relatives or co-workers - they're stuck with you! Ask the people who actively choose to have you in their life - what is it about you that makes them want to spend time with you? These are the same qualities that will make the audience want to hang out with you. These are the very same qualities that will make the director, producer, head of the studio and the network fall in love with (and hopefully hire!) you. So if it's your crazy sense of humor, then I want you to give us a taste of that humor in all of your Series Regular auditions. You may say, but what if I'm going out for a Drama? Well, a drama is simply an hour slice of life - and that includes humor – so you'll bring some levity to the show! You may be thinking "But what if my character just saw someone get killed - there's no place for humor there!" Obviously not, but rarely will the sole audition scene for a Series Regular role have such extreme emotional intensity. That's simply because it doesn't tell us what we really need to know about you. Your character isn't going to be sobbing hysterically on every episode, so how does that scene help us to know who you'll be on the series week after week? If you find yourself with an intensely sad and serious scene, please remember that emotional pain doesn't have to be expressed as a cathartic opera. We're more complex than that - someone who's desperately trying to keep it together can evoke an even greater amount of compassion from the audience. More often than not you can find the hidden levels and colors in the text to organically show us who you are. Give us a glimpse into your persona and what draws people to you. If it's your big heart and empathy, I want to see a bit of that. If it's your incredible smarts, I want to see a bit of that.

One And Done

Episodic roles are trickier. When we're casting Series Regulars, we're looking for Stars. This usually isn't so when we're looking to cast the rest of the episode. With an Under-5 or small Co-Star TV role, you are usually there for exposition. You are there to serve and support the story, so they don't necessarily want someone unique or fascinating unless that's what the role specifically calls for. They aren't looking at you thinking "would I be excited to write for you?" or "does this actor have enough power to engage an audience for 8 years?" They're usually just thinking "Do I believe this actor is a lab technician, construction worker, etc.?" So you don't want arrows pointing at your head saying "hey - look at me!" You want to seamlessly be a part of the episode as the EMT worker or the roommate who witnessed the crime. There's usually no need for them to see anything other than that in you. Most of the time these roles are simply there to move the story along. I say most of the time because you also need to have the foresight to discern whether or not this small role could recur. If the character is the Star's co-worker on the show or lives in the Star's every-day world, then there's always the possibility that you could come back for more episodes. In that instance it's a case-by-case judgment call as to whether or not you give a little something extra, a little pinch of spice, to that audition. To further confuse you, in a Half-Hour Comedy Episodic audition they may or may not want you to be funny, depending on the particular show. Sometimes they just want exposition, sometimes they want funny. I know - I wish it was more cut-and-dried, for all of our sake! Guest Star and some Co-Star roles are larger and will likely require a lot more as these are usually the meat-and-potatoes of the story in an episode. Sometimes these auditions can be done in the same manner as a Series Regular audition, but remember that in this case - unless it's a recurring role - there's no need for them to think about writing for you. What we do need is for you to understand what the character is going through in this story - emotionally and intellectually - and to convey this to us in the audition. This all may sound uber-simplistic to many of you, but you'd be surprised how many good actors just skate through the surface of Guest Star and Co-Star auditions. We've been telling actors for years to be subtle and to not chew up the scenery for Episodics because it's more about telling the story through you than it is about you. That doesn't mean "do nothing." Also, many actors misinterpret the advice we give them for most Under-5 roles of "don't try to stand out, just read it believably" as being for ALL Episodic auditions. Don't confuse an Under-5 that's there as simple exposition for a Guest-Star or Co-Star role that requires a hell of a lot more! To answer your question before you ask it, Film auditions can be any of the above - it depends on what the role is, its function within the movie and who the director is. It truly is an art to discern what is too little and what is too much, but damn — it's also subject to opinion and therefore confusing, I know!

Why Are You Yelling?

Ah, Volume. Volume is one of the few things that can drastically change your audition in an instant. Everyone knows that you have to project to the back of the house when you're doing Theater. This feels very unnatural to many of you at first, but everyone gets used to it after a while. Sometimes a little too used to it. After performing eight shows a week for days, weeks, months or years, it may be difficult to adjust to the natural volume of a Film or TV audition. You may have unwittingly trained yourself to associate acting with "Performing" and performing with "Loud", but for the camera you have to un-train yourself! It's important to be conscious of where you are, what medium you're in and to fill that particular space accordingly. Inappropriate volume usually makes you appear less talented than you are, whether it's too quiet or too loud. That alone should be enough incentive to gain control over it! Every single time I ask an actor on camera to adjust to a more conversational volume, the next take is light-years better than the first. I 'm not saying to go to the other end of the spectrum and whisper either - where is this odd world where everyone either whispers or talks loudly?! Just give us the natural volume that would be appropriate to the situation. If you're having dinner with someone in a scene, there is an intimate, relaxed volume that this requires. When we get excited, angry or passionate about something, our volume naturally raises. If your dialogue is "Everyone get out - the house is on fire!" then by all means, yell!

I Totally Forgot I Was Watching An Actor

Whatever you do in an on-camera audition, we should never feel like you're "performing" for us. You need to create the illusion that we're spying on you. It must be so real that if the door was open and I was walking by, I'd think that you and the reader were simply talking before the audition. A TV/computer monitor and a Film screen are like a looking glass into someone else's life. As the viewer, you never feel like the actors you're watching are doing anything for your sake. It's a voyeuristic experience, observing a brief amount of time in this person's life. All of your great ideas, funny choices and hard work simply won't matter if it looks like you're performing for us. As rudimentary and Acting 101 as this may be, we must always believe you!! If you suspect that you may have strayed a bit from this, then I suggest that you change your perspective in the audition. You're an actor because you love doing this more than anything else you can think of (well, hopefully!). Auditioning is an intrinsic part of acting, so when you're in that room, you're blessed to be doing what you love. Don't forget that you're acting for yourself as much as for anybody else. Think of each audition as you and the reader being immersed in your own little party - "Oh, there's someone else out there? Feel free to join us if you want to - or not - we're having fun here, with or without you!" This will start to dissipate any of the "I'm Performing For You, Powerful Person" habits that you may have picked up.

Go Ahead, Be Bold

This brings me to the age-old, confusing question of being "Too Big" or "Too Small". Some of you with mostly theater credits on your resume are told that your auditions are "Too Big" for camera. You take that to mean that your choices are too bold, so you water down your performance to something that hardly even resembles you anymore. That's not what we want - that's obliterating everything that was special and unique about you in the first place. I think that this is one of the most misunderstood concepts out there. In my book (and this is my book!), the answer is incredibly simple. The criticism of Too Big is grossly misunderstood - there's only believing you or not believing you. Too Big means you're making choices that don't ring true because they aren't coming from an organic place. Possibly you're just talking louder than anyone in real life would in the given situation. We have to believe you - first and foremost!! Nothing you do will mean anything to us if it's not honest. But who said that the definition of "Honest" is "Boring"? This is where "Too Small" comes in. Someone chastised you for being Too Big and so you reduce your rich imagination and choices to a safe, bland broth. Life is filled with honest, crazy emotions and people behave in hysterically funny ways. We can all name great performances in both Comedy and Drama that were incredibly bold, original, BIG and REAL. Show me who you unabashedly are. Big or small, as long as you're coming from a truly authentic place, then you don't have to burden yourself with inhibiting terms like that.

But It Says Here In The Breakdown...

Seeing the Breakdowns or being told about a role from friends has certainly resulted in a few success stories here and there, but for the most part it's not as productive as you would think. The character description in a breakdown can be interpreted in many ways.

Even agents, who understand the criteria of what we're looking for better than most, will many times submit actors that simply aren't what we're looking for. "Cute" in this business really means incredibly attractive, "Beautiful" and "Handsome" means you can't walk down the street without turning heads. "Funny" means someone who can make people laugh even with the most mundane dialogue. The Breakdowns are culled from information in the script, and are written before we've had the benefit of any casting sessions. Although the Breakdown is extremely helpful, the writer, director or producer may develop new ideas about the character along the way. Years ago I was casting a role of the "bitchy best friend" of the star. Of course every actress came in and gave us her most heartfelt bitchy rendition of the character. By the middle of the day, the director turned to me and said "these women are all so *bitchy* - can we get some actresses in here who'll make this character more likeable?" What this invariably means is, "can we get some actresses in here who will make this a three dimensional person and not just a caricature?" Sometimes you get so wrapped up in executing a trait that you know they're looking for that you forget to present a flesh and blood person. Of course, there are exceptions when they actually do want a one dimensional character for a plot device or because it's funny, but don't simply default to that. There are many times when you'll read a character description that you swear is a slam-dunk for you, but the actor they end up hiring is nothing like you. You're just seeing this role through your subjective prism, but be aware that the writer created it through his/her vision and the producer envisions it through his/her vision and the director, network, film or studio executive sees it through his/her vision. If you're allowing the character description to color every choice you make, you may be stifling a more creative and interesting choice. Let me stop here and clarify - I'm not telling you to ignore who the character is or the world they live in. If the role you're auditioning for is a brilliant trial lawyer and a neat-freak, you can't make this character an inarticulate slob. Then you're totally dismissing the writer and trying to be different just for the sake of being different. That's almost as bad as coming in with generic choices or no choices at all because you want them to think of you as a blank canvas -- Eeek! -- that's a painfully boring audition to watch. What I'm saying is, don't put so much energy into fulfilling the character description that you sacrifice something creative and exciting that you might have otherwise brought into the room.

I Swear I Know This!

I touched on this earlier, but one of my biggest pleas to you is for memorization. This is crucial for many reasons, but most importantly because it will free you from what can become "the tyranny of the page". When your attention is stuck on the page, all the energy that could have gone to listening, reacting and creating is tied up in "What's my next line?". You kill a large percentage of your audition this way and you simply can't afford to do that. Another thing to consider is that every time you walk into an audition, you're telling the casting director, producers and director what your work ethic is. Chances are that they don't know you and have no idea how prepared you're going to be (if you're hired) when you show up on the set. If they do know you, it's only wise to stay in their good graces! This is the time to show them how professional you are and how polished your performance will be. Don't think of an audition as a rough facsimile of what you'll do when you get the job - go the distance and do your homework! Walk in as if they've already given you the job and are paying you many thousands of dollars to be here and the cameras are rolling for real. Would you have memorized it better or have spent more time with it then? You have to do it now or the role will likely go to someone who understands the level of preparation we expect. With that said...understand that even though we want it memorized, it's in fact preferable to walk in to an audition with the page in your hand. What you knew backwards in the comfort of your living room has a strange way of flying out of your head when you're actually there in front of people who are judging you. No one wants to see you struggling to remember a line, even if you think that you caught it in time! We would all prefer that you keep the flow of the scene by looking at the page for the dialogue you forgot. So feel free to glance down at the page when you need to, but remember that it's a safety net and not a security blanket! Producers are watching and imagining you in their finished piece - having your eyes glued to the page in your hand potentially ruins that. We have to ask ourselves why you didn't spend more time with the material....do you not care about this job enough? No one wants to hire someone that's disinterested. Some of you have been told that memorization makes you look "cocky" and as if this is the finished product with no room for adjustment. This is beyond ridiculous! No matter what, if you're given an adjustment you must have the ability to switch gears without reservation, but the dialogue is the dialogue and it won't be affected. Even in a situation where the director asks you to improv around the dialogue, having it memorized gives you a solid foundation to jump off from and the ability to play within the existing structure. No one is ever going to fault you for being too professional.

Oops

Now is a good time to talk about flubs and paraphrasing in your audition. Everyone flubs, transposes words and skips text at one time or another. This is where being in the present moment and your improv skills come in. If you were on stage and performing in front of an audience, you wouldn't stop and correct yourself. What would you do? You'd find a way to make whatever you said make sense and maneuver your way back to the scene as seamlessly as possible. You'd want it to appear to the audience as if there was no mistake and that your paraphrase was intended. In an audition, you should do your best to do this as well. There will be times when it's just not feasible – that's perfectly fine. I'm saying to do your best to save it and not just revert to "I'm sorry" or going back to correct your mistake mid-scene. I'm not saying that correcting yourself mid-scene is disastrous, but it certainly takes us out of the scene. If you can make your mistake unnoticeable, we can stay focused on what matters most to us - your personality, how you make the scene flow and how you make the character come to life. It's not the end of the world to us if you transposed a sentence or said the wrong word. It's also a plus to know that you can save a scene if this was to happen on the set – if the scene can be saved, so can money! All of that said, if you're asked to do a second take, please look at your script to see where you flubbed. The first take is fine and forgiven, but saying the same paraphrase the second time around makes us think that you learned it that way. Hmmm. How important is this job to you that you didn't take the time to learn the dialogue correctly? Or do you think your word or phrase is better than the writers? This makes us wonder if you'll ever do the text as written. These aren't the thoughts you want us to have! Words and phrasing are important to the creator, as anyone who's ever been a writer knows. So do whatever you have to in the first take to make everything seem as though it was intended, but get back to the script if you're asked to do it again!

Don't Give Me That Look!

Yes, you are The Actor. Yes, you are the creative force and energy that is needed to make the ink on the page come to life. But never forget that you are being hired to make someone else's (the writer, the director, the producer, the studio or the network) vision materialize, so if they give adjustments to your audition - listen, make the mental adjustment and do it! Be careful that your inner dialogue of "They want what? My choice is so much better" isn't reading on your face! I've seen that

F U look more than a few times and, believe me, it doesn't help you in any way! Whether or not your choice is better isn't the point - do you want this job or not? The older I get, the more I appreciate the wisdom of the question "Do you want to be right or do you want to be happy?" Exceptions notwithstanding, you'll rarely make a good impression by telling them that their choices are essentially inane. Of course, once you have the job you can hopefully collaborate and present your thoughts (in a congenial manner!) to the producers, director, writers, etc. but for the audition the bottom line is - come in with your finished, polished performance but be ready, willing and able to blow your choices to smithereens if they ask you to!

Your Choices Are Everything

Within the perimeters of who the character is and the world that they live in, there are a myriad of choices to make for any audition. I could probably come up with dozens of different choices for any given scene - there never is "one way". So when you come in to the audition, what we're looking for are the choices that you've made. These are not necessarily the choices that the writer put in the stage directions. Whether it's an emotional direction like (Ella sobs uncontrollably) or a physical direction like {John stands up and starts pacing}, if it's not referred to in the dialogue, you don't have to do it. When the dialogue IS WRITTEN IN CAPITALS, THAT MEANS YOU HAVE TO YELL, RIGHT??? Ehhhh...not so much. When you oh-so-carefully color within the lines that way, it may seem like you're giving us what we want but there's also a good chance that you're boring us. We've already seen this same audition countless times, because dozens and dozens of actors are coming in and simply executing what's on the page. When you do that, you're selling us the writer's imagination instead of your own. You're selling us the script, but the writer already sold his/her script – you have to sell yourself! You have to sell us your imagination because,

in the end, that's what we're really buying. If you have an inspiration to do something that's between the lines, we're excited to see that. These are the choices that make your audition different from the fifty people who came in before you and the fifty people who will come in after you. But your choices must come from an organic, authentic place -- never do anything just for the sake of being "different". How many times have I given an actor an adjustment, and they say to me "Oh! That was what I *wanted* to do, but it said in the script to do XYZ...." Always remember that, as an actor, the most valuable asset you have is your unique way of interpreting the world around you. Don't get so caught up in what you think they want that you lose your extraordinary self in the process.

> *"Always be a first-rate version of yourself,*
> *instead of a second-rate version of*
> *somebody else."*
> *- Judy Garland*

There are many, many choices that are legitimate and conceivably right for any given scene. The choices "they" want depend on who the particular director, writers or producers are for this project. There's no way that you can know for certain, preparing in the solace of your living room, what those choices are. You are not a mind reader. Let's say you have an audition scene that's a knock-down, drag-out fight on the page. You walk into the casting office and you're told "we don't want you to play it angry". How in the world would you know that? The answer is - you wouldn't. And don't think that these directions are given by crazy people, because they most certainly aren't! Sometimes a choice that appears to be antithetical to what's obvious on the page can illustrate the story and intentions in a fresher and more fascinating way. Directors are hired for their unique vision just like actors, but you

can't possibly know what his/her vision is before you've even walked in the room. So don't lower your immune system worrying about what choices "they" want to see. Look inside and ask yourself what choices are best to showcase YOU. What does that mean? It means possibly rethinking how you look at your auditions. If you were a producer casting a film, play or TV show that needed charismatic and engaging actors, would you cast yourself? Too many actors walk into an audition only thinking about serving the text. Every choice they make is solely for the greater good of the scene. I'm not saying that you shouldn't serve the text - that would be ridiculous - but I AM saying there are many ways to serve the text, so choose wisely, Grasshopper! If you're auditioning for a sitcom, you want the audience to like you. So within the many choices that you've deemed correct for the scene, pick the ones that will make you the most likable. Choosing something else may very well be a good and defendable choice for the scene, but it's probably not going to make anyone hire you. With few exceptions, everyone in a sitcom is likable. Even the mean, irascible boss or the ruthless social-climber has got to be someone that you love to hate. The operative word there is "LOVE"! There was a television show decades ago named "Hogan's Heroes" where *the Nazi's* were lovable. I mean, really, where do you go from there? For a television pilot, the audience has to love watching you or else they won't tune in every week. And please don't think that "likable" means smiling and never being negative, sad or mad. There are plenty of fights in comedy, but usually (with exceptions) playing end-of-your-rope frustration is going to be more likable than I-hate-your-guts anger in an audition. In the end, this is the ENTERTAINMENT business, and stars are simply people that other people want to watch. It's not beauty that makes a star - otherwise every model would be starring in Films, TV and Theater. It's not acting talent that makes a star - otherwise, you would already be one (come on, isn't that what you were just thinking?!). It's a unique, charismatic quality that is

translated onto the big screen, TV or stage that makes a star - along with a lot of patience, fortitude and a sprinkling of destiny or luck. Oh - and if they're a great actor as well, BONUS!

For Crying Out Loud, Spend More Time With The Material!

We see everything you do, and we see everything that you don't do. Too many times I'll see an actor let entire lines go by where they have no opinion about what they've just said. I can't think of many instances in life where you have no opinion whatsoever about what you're thinking or saying -- why should that be any different when you're acting? Think of the most innocuous thing to talk about -- let's say the weather. You may just be making conversation but in actuality you do have an opinion about it. "It's raining" can mean it makes you feel romantic or depressed or simply that you have to rethink your plans. "It's going to be 90 today" - does that make you feel wilted and miserable or fill you with summertime glee? The crux of your audition, what makes your audition unique, is your personal view of the world. More than anything else, you are being hired for the choices that you make in that 3 minute (or so) audition. Learn to look at scenes through a different prism. If you're faced with a role that is unlikable on the page, is there a way to make yourself someone they'll love to hate as opposed to just hate? That's much more fun to watch. If you've got a scene that's basically just a domestic fight, do you think that the audience just wants to watch you yelling? How about showing a bit of what's underneath the anger -- the hurt, the disappointment? That's much more sympathetic, identifiable and three dimensional. Don't make the mistake that a whopping 80% of actors make by executing only what's on the page and stopping there. We already know what's on the page -- the writer wrote it and the producer, director and I have already read and seen it. Many times. Show us what's

not there. Make it even better than we thought it was on the page. Make it yours.

Self-Taping...a Great Opportunity or a Waste of Time

Whether you're out of town, on another job (yay!) or the casting director simply has no time to see you, self-taping can be a great way to be considered for a role that you wouldn't otherwise be able to audition for. Sadly, many of the self-tapes that I receive are virtually unusable due to mistakes that can (for the most part) be easily corrected.

1. Watch your audition before you send it!! Think of yourself as the producer who is watching and imagining you on their TV show or in their film. This is the ballpark we're aiming for. Although you won't have the same quality camera or lighting that you would in a professional setting, you should try to make it look as good as possible. I've actually seen great looking auditions that were done on iPhones, so no excuses! Try to avoid heavy shadows on your face (unless looking older and less attractive than you are is your goal!) Remember to dress appropriately for the character - just because you're at home or in your trailer doesn't mean we'll overlook your jammies or moth-eaten sweater. Many actors tend to forget that this is ultimately being watched with the same critical eye as all of the in-person auditions.

2. Do a test shot to see how you look. When you sit too close to the recording device, your face looks slightly distorted. A good general guide is to frame yourself from your hips/waist up if it's a comedy and a bit closer (from your waist/top-ribs up) if it's a drama. There shouldn't be much discernible space above your head – the frame should ideally sit at or near the top of your crown. I can't begin to count the number of self-tapes I get where the actor is at the bottom third of the screen! Try to

give us a straight-on image, not angled up or angled down. If someone else is manning the camera, this will be much easier, but do the best that you can. Give us one standing full-body (or as much of yourself as you can get in there) shot and tell us your height so that we'll have an accurate image of what you look like.

3. Please try to avoid reading with yourself, using a recorder to recite the other role back to you. It's distracting, a bit odd, and the timing on those solo-recorded auditions can be a painful thing to watch! There's usually a friend within pleading distance that you can ask. Of course we always prefer that you have a competent actor reading with you, but anyone is better than no one! If the placement of the reader makes them a lot louder than you, simply ask them to speak in a quieter tone.

4. If possible, do your audition against a plain wall or a place that isn't so distracting that we're reading the book titles on the shelf!

5. Do two different takes if you're uncertain about the tone of a scene, but post your favorite one first.

6. Just like any in-person audition, your reading should be so honest that we feel like voyeurs watching you. Keep your volume in the correct, organic place for the space and the scene. It shouldn't seem like you're "performing" for us, except in the rare case where that's what's required.

7. Please, I beg you - send your hard work to us in a form that is quick and easy to download. I would like to give you examples, but technology changes on a daily basis so by the time you read this the recommendations will be different! Understand that casting directors are usually very pressed for time and get frustrated waiting for a download that takes too long to complete. Some don't even want to type in a password - not

because they're lazy, but because they've been given the wrong or expired password one too many times!

I see more actors get jobs through self-taping these days than ever before...take the time to do it the right way and hopefully you'll be one of them!

Subjectivity (Opinions Are Like Pie-holes...Everybody Has One)

Being cast in a role rarely comes down to the fact that you can act the part -- there are literally hundreds of actors that could arguably do it as well as you. It's not simply about your look or your type -- there are scores of people out there who look like your fraternal twin. There are times when it's not even about your skill as an artist. Casting ultimately is about an actor's essence, and the people on the hiring end are coming from a very subjective perspective regarding exactly what essence they're looking for. This is usually a group of very diverse personalities that will have to agree that you are the answer. Because the casting director is compiling the list of actors, they're the first ones that must believe you're right for the role. I'm not dissing all the great agents and managers out there that push their actors to us – many times they are the unsung heroes in all of this. But the fact is that the casting director is the first really influential line of defense that you have to get through. We are just regular folk, in case you haven't noticed, with all of the baggage and personal opinions that come along with being human. We have all been wrong about an actor at one time or another. We have all had the experience of resisting an agent or manager about seeing someone who ultimately got the part once we gave in. More often than not, though, we've been right (or we wouldn't keep our jobs!). We've all been known to plead our case to producers for an actor we passionately believe in who ultimately got the job. But despite our varying degrees of influence on the project, we are not the ones to decide who gets the role. I've been in countless TV, film and theater casting sessions with a room full of Those In A Position To Hire You, all of whom have their own taste, perspective and personal lives in there with them. You walk in, you do your audition and you leave. One of them loves you and wants to hire you there and then. One thinks you're totally wrong for this and says your laugh annoyed them. Oh, and we're not even bringing sex appeal into this - you can only imagine how diverse opinions can be when that's part of the criteria! Now, I don't want to make it sound like your talent has nothing to do with it. In the majority of instances you will get somewhere in this business (notice I didn't specify where) based on how good you are. But never forget that the people on the other side of the room are simply human. They come to this with the same subjectivity that you yourself have when you judge things - the strangers you meet, your friends, your family, the food you eat, the novels you read and the movies that you think are great or crap.

So You Had A Bad Day

What should you do if you give a lousy audition for a casting director or producer that doesn't know you well? You're having a bad day or just not connecting with the material, but either way you know that you didn't do well in there. Or maybe you thought you did a great job in there but the feedback that your agent gets is dismal. You might say "But it was Important-Person's-Name!" "But there are only a finite number of casting directors and I screwed it up"! You can berate yourself, freak out and be depressed, but I honestly believe that your fate simply didn't lie with that particular person. You can't and won't be everyone's cup of tea, no matter how good you are. But you don't need everyone. All it takes is that one person who believes in you and that one job that takes you to the next level.

Try to get something that you can use constructively from the feedback, because this may very well be your key to that next level. If not, this may simply be a lesson in how to develop a thicker skin and keep your faith in yourself. Don't blow the occasional misstep out of proportion, just learn what you can from it and move on.

Our greatest glory consists not in never falling,
but in rising every time we fall.
- Oliver Goldsmith

CHAPTER 3:

THE ART OF MARKETING YOURSELF : WHO YOU ARE (AND WHY WE WANT TO KNOW)

The Internal Stuff

We are all incredibly different and we are all incredibly similar. There are many people who look a lot like you and even more who are "your type". There are many people who share your sense of humor, world view or personal taste. We are all part of one huge tapestry - all connected and more alike than Governments would like us to know and Yankees / Red Sox fans would have us think. But no one else has the exact same thought process or sees life in the exact same way as you do. How could they? Information and experience, no matter how universal, gets filtered through your unique sieve. You're a magical mixture of your personal influences, upbringing, dramas, traumas, epiphanies and DNA -- and so there is truly only one You.

That makes you fascinating. Why don't you trust that? I believe that the single biggest mistake that you can make as an actor is not showing us who YOU are. Ultimately, when we've determined that you can act and that you meet whatever external requirements might be needed for a role, it really gets down to Who You Are. Some actors innately understand this, but many don't.

When you're in class or have recently graduated from an acting program, you've spent a lot of time doing scene study, movement, etc. Training can be a wonderful thing. Be it Grad School or a

Meisner class, acquiring tools or sharpening those that you already have can be enormously beneficial to you. The problem comes when you can't differentiate learning devices in class from the things you should carry with you into the day-to-day professional world.

I can't begin to count the number of actors that I audition who see the character as a foreign entity outside of themselves rather than seeing the character as a relatable extension of themselves. I'm not talking about someone's personal acting process here, I'm talking about something on an even grander scale. It's the philosophical question of "I" as a Being that's separate from the world or "I" as part of the fabric of the world. However you choose to see it, we are all connected. Whether you like it or not, most of us have the same basic physical processes, male/female plumbing, the same need for food, water and shelter. Almost everyone desires good health and love (be it romantic, spiritual or existential). There's a lot of speculation about what the most important thing in life is. Many people say "Health - without your health, you have nothing." Others say "Love. Without love you have nothing." Both extremely valid philosophies, but I never liked the fact that if I embraced one answer it implied that I was giving up the other.... what is this, "Sophie's Choice"? I prefer my Dad's answer, even though I rejected it as an 11 year old as too simplistic (when I was simultaneously too old and too young to accept the enormous wisdom of simplicity). My Dad always said that everyone, everywhere basically wants the same thing. "We all just want to be happy". OK, that I buy. Think about it - if you're happy, that more or less takes care of everything. My cynical/wiseass friends might counter "What if NOT being happy makes me happy?" To which I say "...whatever makes you happy!"

But I digress.

It's an indisputable fact that as different as we may be, there are also many universal truths that we all share. Thinking of a character as someone "other" can potentially cut you off from the deeper understanding that you get when you think of the character, and all humanity for that matter, as a part of you. If you're playing a street hooker or a homeless person, it's one-dimensional and condescending to simply play the stereotype. There's more honesty in connecting to that person as someone that could have been you, had your life presented very different and much more challenging circumstances. There but for the grace of God go any one of us.

Of course there are those who would strongly disagree with this philosophy of acting - that's valid, as there is never, ever one answer for anything. This is simply what I have culled over years and years of observation, direction, discussion and contemplation. Everyone has to come to their own conclusions.

Great power for an actor is to be accessible and identifiable. What makes an actor watchable and desirable is his/her ability to make a connection with the audience, to share and illuminate the private moments that we all have. To represent the audience in their life journey through your character's journey. You do this by accessing the eternal human truth within yourself.

Don't fool yourself into thinking that any human condition or experience is so foreign to you. You can certainly use some of the goodies found outside but you are The Source, always - and you are so damn interesting – so why not start there?

> *"Go to thy bosom - knock there, and ask your heart what it doth know"*
>
> *- Shakespeare*

Some External Stuff (hey, let's face it, this is the business we're in)

Everyone has many different sides to their personality. Just because we think of you as "The Charming Guy" doesn't mean we'll never bring you in for "The Bad Guy". "Type" simply means how we would most readily cast you.

In the end, a casting director is going to call you in for what they think you're right for, regardless of what you think. Sometimes, we call in people against type because, under the right circumstances, that can be a fresh and creative way to cast a role.

If you've never given much thought to your "type" and you're doing just fine, go ahead and skip this. If it ain't broke, don't fix it!

However, many actors over the years have come to me totally distressed over this dilemma..... "Can you tell me what my type is"?

If you were selling me cookies that you had made, would you ask me what kind they are? If you were selling me a book you had written, would you ask me what it's about? We expect you to know who you are and what you've got to offer better than we do, but that's not always the case. Being self-aware enough to know if you're funny or not, conventionally beautiful or not, etc. is terribly important in helping you navigate this journey. We all know someone who is very adept at analyzing other people but can't manage to see themselves at all. When someone that's in this space has an epiphany and starts seeing themselves honestly, their entire world can open up. When you're insightful enough to know who you are, your ability to find and convey meaning through the dialogue in a script can exponentially increase.

You really should know at least two basic things about yourself:

I - What do you look like?

Let's start with what SHOULD be obvious to an actor, but for some reason rarely is. Be realistic about your looks. I'd say a good 50% of actors that I question about this are not seeing themselves clearly. You think you should be a leading man or leading woman? Okay, look at the people who have those roles on TV and in Films. Most are widely considered to be conventionally, even stunningly beautiful.

This is very rare among the human population. I don't care what your scorecard with the ladies is or how many guys you've dated. This is simply a different criteria. I love that your Mom gave you confidence by gushing over how gorgeous you are. Your significant other loves you and should believe that you're the most beautiful thing ever. I truly, truly believe that everybody's beautiful in their own way, just like that sweet and cheesy 70's song says. But in this business, there's an undeniable standard for conventional beauty and it is what it is. Just Google "The 10 Most Handsome/Beautiful Actors/Actresses" - this is the bar by which everyone else is judged. But not every leading man/woman is as physically perfect as these examples, and that's where the wiggle room for confusion and subjective interpretation comes in. People may either overestimate or underestimate their attractiveness. Be as honest as possible with yourself, without the embarrassment of feeling egotistical or the armor of false confidence.

When you see yourself clearly externally, you may be better able to see yourself clearly internally...and vice-versa!

2 - What are your outstanding traits?

If you're having trouble discerning what your type is, write down at least 5 words or traits that you would use to describe yourself. Then enlist the help of your most supportive yet constructively honest friends, siblings, etc. asking them to describe your personality in a few adjectives. If you're not defensive and your ego is ready for this, let them see your description of yourself and discuss your agreements and disagreements. This will probably become a bit of a therapy session, so be sure that you're receptive to and mindful about whom you enlist! This isn't meant to ruin your friendships so make sure that your ego can handle a discussion about your character and physicality! You may be pleasantly surprised about some perceptions and you may be perturbed about others, but as an actor you can only grow. You'll come out of this with a clearer idea of how others see you - which is every bit as helpful in this business as how you see yourself. This in turn gives you a better idea of what is considered "your type".

How do these traits fit into different roles? Are you etherial and vulnerable? Don't expect to be seen for many cop roles. Are you shy and introspective? The 1/2 hour comedies aren't going to be thrown at your feet. Do you have a strong command of the English language and a smart, persuasive presence? Hello lawyer roles! Are you a friendly, nurturing woman in her mid to late 30's? Hey Mom, what's for dinner?

Understanding what your type is can help you to polish specific aspects of yourself that will make you more employable. I've seen many sexy actresses come into auditions with baggy clothes and minimal makeup. There are bubbly, extremely fun people who flatten their personalities out totally once they begin acting. We need to see who you are. Just like the old adage "You can't love someone else until you love yourself first", it's also true that we can't know who you are until you know yourself first.

Every type is represented in Film, TV and Theater these days - every age, race and body type. Gone are the homogenous days of just a few decades ago – thankfully - but there is always room for improvement. Being conventionally beautiful or handsome is only necessary if you're up for a role that requires this. Cultivating your own brand of attractiveness is really the key, because the reality is that we live in a world that prefers attractive to unattractive. But what exactly does "attractive" mean? An average looking guy who's funny and charming is ultimately more attractive than the humorless, dull hunk. A woman with imperfect features but lots of style and confidence can be so much more attractive than someone with classic looks but no sense of self. So why should you care about superficial things like hair and makeup? If they hire you, they'll have professional hair, makeup and wardrobe people to make you look great - right? If you really think that you can get a Series Regular role that way, you're sadly mistaken. However, for Episodic TV, Film or Theater, it all depends on the requirements for that particular role. Bottom line - understand what's expected of you in whatever arena you're auditioning for and come in with it! Which brings us to....

Notes For The Ladies

There can be larger responsibilities for a woman coming in to an audition than for a man. Men (generally) don't have expectations put upon them regarding makeup and hair. This is simply a reflection of our society as a whole. The pursuit of external beauty is the sometimes delightful and sometimes burdensome albatross that keeps women buying billions of dollars of cosmetics every year. Advertising isn't confined to commercials - we buy into a standard of beauty that's put in front of us on TV, the Internet, in Film and in Fashion magazines. There are many books devoted to the Why's of our Western views on this, so I'm not going to even attempt to solve it here. Not every successful actress is "beautiful" in the culturally accepted way, but they all understand exactly how to look their personal best. The majority of my world in Casting centers on Network TV Series Regulars. These are the stars of the show that are on every week, or at least the majority of the episodes aired. With very few exceptions (remember, there are ALWAYS exceptions!), these roles require that you come in to the audition looking your personal best. Of course we can all name some Cable and New Media series that don't require anything more in grooming than brushing your teeth, but that's a whole other ballgame for now. For most Series Regular gigs, consider how you would spend a long time on your hair and makeup when going out on a hot date -- you don't want to look like you're trying too hard, but you want to look great. If you're a klutz with a blow-dryer, get lessons from your stylist. If you don't have great makeup skills, get lessons from a makeup artist. These are tax deductible items as an actor, so no excuses! The difference in how you'll look and feel will definitely be noticeable, and you need every bit of confidence you can get. I've had actresses say "but this role is a Cop" or "in this scene she's just in the supermarket". Well, show me the Network Series Regular Cop that doesn't have her eyeliner and lip-gloss....show me the Series Regular strolling through the supermarket with crappy looking hair. I'm not talking about having to measure up to that standard of beauty here - there are many roles that don't require the Size 2 Gorgeous Girl. I'm talking about looking your own personal best. I'm talking about coming in as the After Picture. Do you think that you can audition without concern for your hair and makeup because we can imagine what you'll look like after a team of stylists have worked their magic on you? Whether we can or cannot, with the stakes this high no one wants to "imagine" anything. If you get this job, they're banking a lot on you - they're saying that you are potentially a star. They have to see what they're getting, right in front of them, in order to commit to you. Unless you're already a well-known actor, the audition is the only place to show them what you'll bring to the table - the unique way that you interpret the role, your strong work ethic and what you will look like on the show. There's very little room for guesswork!

A Note For The Guys

Well, you do have it easier than the ladies, but you're not completely off the hook. Do you see most Series Regulars with pimples? Dark circles under their eyes? Shiny foreheads? The answer (unless it's done for a specific storyline) is NO! So don't come in that way! These guys don't all have perfect skin, but they all sit in a make-up chair before any filming starts! No, no, no, I'm not saying to wear mascara to bring out your eyes or anything like that – I'm saying get some concealer, some powder or oil absorbing blotting tissues and learn how to use them correctly. It should never look like you're wearing any makeup at all, so it's important that you do it correctly. If you have any of the above skin issues, have a makeup savvy friend or a professional makeup artist help you pick out the right shade of powder or concealer and teach you how to apply it. Do you think that's asinine? Here's a better question – Do you want this job?

In case you're still in doubt, I'll give you this to chew on : There was an actor who was absolutely perfect for a role and knocked it out of the park in his audition. The feedback was "We love him, but his forehead is shiny and we can't commit to him unless we see him without a shiny forehead". The actor comes back in with powder on his forehead, he does the same audition sans shine, and thankfully he gets the job. SO - what am I telling you? No one wants to rely on guesswork when there are Imax screens and 60 inch HD TV's out there! The stakes are very high at this point and you have to walk in there at 110%. Don't go into an on camera audition for a leading role with a shiny forehead, dark circles or pimples unadorned for all to see! Again, I'm talking about leading roles here and there are always exceptions to everything…but I'm just sayin'.

Either Gender

Episodic roles are the day players and guest roles. You're there for a day or possibly the length of an episode but you are not the star, so the way you should look for the audition depends on the role. This pretty much holds true for Film auditions as well. If you're going out for the one scene Beat Cop, all they want to see is your average, everyday Beat Cop. If you're auditioning for a Salesperson at Saks 5th Avenue, you want to dress and appear differently than you would for a Clerk at a roadside convenience store. Always dress in the world that the character lives in. but rarely should it seem like you just came from the Costumer - we don't want you in scrubs for a Doctor. Just give us the impression that you live in that world. If you're auditioning for a white collar professional, like a Lawyer, at least wear a jacket if not a suit. The actor that comes in for that role in a tee shirt runs a high risk of being dismissed as "not a lawyer". Many years ago I was casting a role of a homeless guy and brought in a very good actor that came in clean cut and dressed as he normally would be. The response was that he wasn't right for the part. I asked the actor to come back in two days and not shave or comb his hair in the interim. When he came back in, we rumpled him up a bit more and – voila! – he got the role. Don't leave these things to chance. It's your responsibility to give us little-to-no speculation regarding your audition. Casting is immensely important to the director and producers but they've got a LOT on their plate. They're dealing with sets, locations, notes to the writers, etc., etc., so they don't always have the time to fill in the blanks that you've left out of your audition.

The Bottom Line: Don't make us rely on guesswork. Show us that you live in the character's world from the moment you step in the room. Are there ever exceptions to this? Once again, there are exceptions to everything!

CHAPTER 4:

ANXIETY, NERVOUSNESS AND STAGE FRIGHT - WHAT TO DO ABOUT IT

"Never let the fear of striking out get in your way."

- Babe Ruth

To my knowledge, the majority of actors get nervous before an audition or a performance. This is nothing to worry about unless it stops you from doing your best. Sometimes the anxiety goes away as experience and confidence take over, and sometimes it never goes away. Sid Caesar, one of the most famous and loved comedians of the 1950's and 60's, used to throw up from nerves before he went out on stage for his weekly live TV Show. No less than Sir Lawrence Olivier suffered for years from stage fright.

I think that the first step in taming this gnarly little beast is to understand the root of your fear. It's understandably ironic that some people become actors for the very same reason that causes their performance anxiety – the need to be loved. Wanting to be loved is a positive, beautiful thing. Needing to be loved, however, can open you up to all sorts of fear. Your fear may come from the belief that you aren't enough just as you are. Do you need the outside approval of others before you feel any self-worth? Maybe you fear that no one will love you if you "fail". I'm not saying it's easy, as the psyche of an actor can be complex. Most of you are vulnerable to outside influences - you have to be in order to respond and be open to another actor's energy in a scene. Ah, but there are two sides to this coin. This same vulnerability can also make your self-esteem too dependent on external validation. You're constantly being judged, whether you're just starting out or you're an "A List" star. No matter how great you are, there will always be somebody out there who is not a fan. This is just a fact that you have to learn to live with. So what does this mean? That everything you know about yourself and your talent is a lie? No, it simply means that everything is subjective and therefore all that matters is what YOU think about yourself. If someone says they hate anchovies but you love them, would that make you doubt your taste and stop eating anchovies? This may sound silly, but it's a valid point! I believe that the first and most important step in getting over nervousness as an actor is trusting and believing in yourself MORE than you trust and believe in the precarious opinion of others. If someone outside of yourself is responsible for giving you your self-worth, then you are also giving them the power to take it away. Putting so much weight on external validation and external prizes diminishes the greatest feeling of all - your own validation and self-love. Why did you become an actor in the first place? You had to believe in yourself enough to reject all of the safer, more lucrative professions that you could have chosen. So the key is to come into every audition and performance with that same belief. If you can do this while being 110% prepared (as I talked about in the previous chapters), then some people may love your talent and some may not – but most importantly you'll feel confidence and love within yourself.

Therapy, religion and/or self-help books are all possible tools to help get you to this calmer Zen place, but everyone responds to different approaches. Here are some other ideas that have worked for various actors:

Let's Try the Healthy Route First

I'm not a huge fan of rushing to ingest any external substance for emotional issues. Everything has its place, but blindly reaching for a pill to get rid of your Audition Anxiety is usually just a band-aid. I believe that there is a more profound, if slower, route that may ultimately guide you in ways that no pill ever can. There are so many friendly, healthful and valuable tools out there to help you with these paralyzing emotions. A few of these involve changing bad habits and making lifestyle changes. Others are simpler and require no "sacrifices" from you. You're the only one who knows if you're ready to take a step like this towards wholeness. Whatever you choose, you may be surprised at how effective some of these may be:

Just Say No (don't whine, your body will thank you!)

Avoidance of aggravating substances can be a huge step in the right direction. Simply (or not so simply!) avoiding sugar, excess alcohol, gluten, dairy products (bye-bye cheese!), caffeine and tobacco will help you in a myriad of ways – one of them being your nervous system. I assume that everyone is aware of the negative impact that alcohol has on your emotions. Every crappy feeling that this chapter is about is exacerbated by alcohol, to say the least. Caffeine seems benign in comparison, but it can sure pack a nasty punch. There have been numerous studies linking caffeine with anxiety and insomnia. Caffeine isn't just in coffee - it's hiding in chocolate (argggh!), black tea, certain medications and many sodas. Green tea and white tea both have caffeine in a milder form so they may not affect you in such a negative way. Both caffeine and tobacco are stimulants, and stimulants release adrenaline into your bloodstream. Adrenaline can cause many of the symptoms of panic, fear and anxiety. Sugar is another stimulant that can be a major cheerleader for these negative emotional attacks. It causes a massive swing in insulin levels which can ultimately lead to our buzz word anxiety and its fun cousin, depression. Gluten grains like wheat, barley, oats and rye are difficult for many people to digest. The gelatinous buildup of gluten protein in the blood can cause an over-excitement of brain cells which leads to – you guessed it – anxiety. All dairy products create inflammation in the body, which in turn can cause many problems – including the A word. I know, I know - these are all comfort substances and not easy for most people to give up! There are studies that say sugar is as addictive as heroin or cocaine. Maybe you can take baby-steps and try avoiding these potential triggers for a day or two. Experiment on the weekend, when there is little chance of getting an audition, to see if you have any major withdrawal symptoms. If you do, know that they will dissipate the longer your body is free of this very toxic substance. Your level of motivation will probably be in direct proportion to your level of frustration and disgust with your situation!

Hey, At Least You'll Smell Great

Essential oils are a subtle and pretty safe (unless you're allergic) way to influence your mood. You can dilute a few drops of any of the following relaxing essential oils in a carrier oil such as olive oil, almond oil, jojoba oil - most vegetable, seed or nut oils that you find pleasant can be used. Try Essential oils of Chamomile, Lavender, Rose, Clary Sage, Ylang Ylang, Jasmine, Lemonbalm, Neroli or Sandalwood –whichever combination of scents pleases you the most. You can buy a 4 oz. dark blue or amber bottle in most stores that sell essential oils. The dark bottle is so the volatile oils won't degrade or go rancid. Mix 40 drops of essential oil (a combination of 2 or more that you like of the above) with enough carrier oil to almost fill the bottle. You can use this as a massage oil or a bath oil. If you hate the feel of oil on your body, just add a few drops of essential oil to any moisturizing lotion and massage it into your skin. You can also put these oils into a diffuser and breathe in the calming effects. By the way, essential oils work because of the effect that inhaling them has on the brain, not because of their absorption through your skin.

Meditation (too much blahblahblah in my head)
We've all heard about the benefits of Meditation, but I know very few people who actually have the time or discipline to apply this ancient practice to their life. Those that do are some of the most focused and successful actors that I know. Am I saying that Meditation is responsible for that? Maybe, maybe not, but it certainly helps! If you find the concept of keeping your body and mind still for long periods of time daunting, join the club. My mind has so much monkey-chatter that Meditation is simply a time when I can think about all the things that I'm usually too busy to think about! I'm (half) kidding, but there are a few accessible forms that have worked well for me. You may want to give this one a shot before throwing this extremely valuable practice aside entirely:

The Relaxation Response was formulated by Herbert Benson, M.D. in the 1970's. After studying practitioners of Transcendental Meditation, he found that they could lower their blood pressure, heart rate, oxygen consumption and slow their breathing at will. Being a man of science, he removed the religious aspects of TM and distilled it down to its basic component - putting all thoughts out of your mind except for the repetition of a single sound, word or phrase. Hey, it costs nothing and may be worth a try the next time you're feeling nervous before an audition or a job. This is how it works:

1. Find a place to sit where you will be undisturbed for 10 minutes (the casting director's office bathroom with multiple stalls seems like a logical place!).
2. Close your eyes and relax any muscles that feel tense.

3. Breathe very slowly through your nose and exhale very slowly through your mouth. As you exhale, think or silently say a word or phrase that makes you feel calm -- it could be a no-brainer like "Relax", "I am relaxed", "Peace" or "I am peaceful". It could be an affirmation like "I am a great actor" or "I am enough just as I am". It can be something religious like The Serenity Prayer - there's no right or wrong here, just whatever works for you.

4. If sounds around you disturb your concentration (or make you laugh, if you're in the bathroom!) just make a mental note of that and bring your thoughts back to your breathing, your word, your phrase.

5. At the end of whatever time you've allotted for this, take a few inhales and exhales as you bring the outside world back into your consciousness and slowly open your eyes. Gradually get up.

Ideally, they say you should do this four times a week to get the full benefits, but even if you only do it when you're stressed it may help.

Sleep

Everyone knows how important sleep is, and it's especially true for an actor. Without the proper amount of sleep, you're not going to be as mentally sharp as you can be. That obviously can affect your audition or your performance. Not being at the top of your game is detrimental to anyone's profession, but an actor has even more to be concerned about. You look like crap when you're tired - puffy, baggy eyes, sallow skin - yeah, that's really attractive. This is even more worrisome if you're filming something that will one day be in a movie theater or displayed on a 52 inch HD TV! A lot of discipline is required to get in bed early – even if you do, some nights it may be difficult to fall asleep. Prescription drugs, in my opinion, do much more harm than good and have yet to prove otherwise; supplements are much safer but anything ingested has the potential to affect you negatively... so more on this later in the chapter! A safe and effective option you can try is a kind of Meditation for the Body. Progressive Relaxation is something I discovered as a little kid when I couldn't fall asleep. This technique really works like a charm for me when it's 2:00 am and I'm wide awake:

1. The room should be dark. Lying on your back, make yourself as comfortable as possible. Sometimes putting a pillow under your knees puts your body in a comfortable alignment.

2. Close your eyes.

3. Concentrate on your toes. The very tips of your toes. Relax them to the point where they're almost floating. There's no rush.

4. Concentrate on the balls of your feet. Relax them to the point where they're almost floating. Take your time.

5. Concentrate on the arches of your feet. Relax them to the point where they're almost floating. Take your sweet time.

6. Concentrate on your heels. Relax them to the point where they're almost floating. Take your ever-lovin' sweet time.

....and on and on and up and up until you eventually, eventually get to the top of your head. I've never gotten that far because I'm always asleep by then!

Other Ways To Show Yourself You Care

There are other methods to quiet your performance anxiety like EFT (Emotional Freedom Technique) which are designed to give you the tools to deal with stress when and where you need them. I can't be a staunch advocate for EFT at this point because I haven't used it enough myself, but it seems to be an exciting and relatively easy practice. I know many people that swear it works like nothing else. Basically an emotional acupuncture technique, you lightly tap specific meridian points on your body while thinking about and/or saying affirmations regarding your specific problem. I'm told that it works wonders for negative behavior and thought patterns like fear, anxiety, sadness and anger. There's a ton of information on EFT on the internet if you're interested in learning more. From its success rate, I suspect that this technique will become more known and widely used in the coming decades.

Exercise in any form is great to help you feel your best, both psychologically and physiologically. A less toxic body means a less toxic mind. The trick is to find what works best for you, from Pilates to Karate. Stretching is an important component of any form of exercise. Stretching can relieve stress and release constricting emotions in your body. This isn't an exercise book, so I'm not going to go into the many forms that you can do. I will, however, touch on the ancient, tried and true method of Yoga. A regular Yoga practice will definitely help to burn off anxiety - it's no wonder that so many actors are into it. Yes, some forms are about flexibility and twisting yourself into a pretzel - but if that's not for you, there are many different types of Yoga. Some are very intense and detoxifying like Bikram where the room is 105 degrees (I'm growing faint just typing that) and some are very easy, calming and relaxing like Restorative Yoga. Not all Yoga is about holding poses forever or going so quickly that you feel like you were thrown into a Broadway Musical without knowing the choreography! Don't be so quick to say it isn't for you - there's usually a form that will serve your needs. Specific breathing techniques are an integral part of any Yoga practice. Long, deep breathing - where the exhale is twice as long as the inhale - is especially beneficial for stress. If you can't get to a class or money is tight, there are a lot of great DVD's to try. My personal favorites are the Kundalini series by

Ravi Singh and Ana Brett. They really make Yoga fun and always emphasize the mind-body connection of what you're doing. Most of the workouts can be done by almost anyone (I say that because I can do them!). I have no affiliation with these people whatsoever, I just love when something is done so well! Whatever you choose to do, be very aware that you can injure yourself doing Yoga as easily as you could with any other exercise, so proceed with caution! I would never advise starting something new without getting a professional instructor to help you in the beginning. I gave myself a torn meniscus, a shoulder injury and a pulled back muscle, which were the direct result of my stupidity in barreling ahead without preliminary instruction - that kind of says it all!

Hydrotherapy - everything from soaking in an Epsom Salts bath to a Jacuzzi. I'd give my left testicle (if I had one) for a daily Jacuzzi.

Massage is a fantastic way to relax - but who has the money to get them as often as we need them? Although they're detoxifying and nothing makes you more relaxed than a long soak in the tub and a massage, these aren't exactly the most practical solutions for the specific challenge of stage fright or anxiety in an audition. I mention them only because they are great adjuncts in training yourself to calm down!

Music therapy - music can have a profound effect on one's mood....if there's specific music that inspires or eases you, by all means bring it with you to your auditions. Just keep your iPod volume low enough as to not invade your fellow auditioner's concentration. Having your own personal theme music can both empower and soothe you. I wonder if street aggression has dissipated at all since the inception of iPods and MP3 players?

Journaling - When I was 12 and had more life-challenges than a 12 year old should really have, I wrote all my thoughts and fears down in a notebook. I concentrated mostly on my worries and what the worst possible outcome could be. I just did automatic writing - I didn't think about grammar, spelling or censoring my thoughts - I just wrote and wrote. I always, ALWAYS felt so much better afterwards. One reason was because I was expressing my feelings unabashedly and without any concern about someone else's perception (because no one else would ever read it). An even bigger reason, perhaps, was because the answer to "what's the worst thing that could happen?" always turned out to be less scary than I had imagined once it was down on paper. This method got me through my formative years (along with reading books by Dr. Wayne Dyer) and into my 20's without any need for a therapist. I'm not advocating that for anyone else, I'm just illustrating that journaling is a powerful and free tool that may be very helpful to you. If you're anxious and afraid before or during auditions, I would try writing down your feelings and fears. What's the worst thing that could happen in the audition? That whoever is judging you won't like you and think that you're not a good actor? Oh, well - then your destiny doesn't lie with that person. There's always someone else out there and all it takes is one job to suddenly get everyone interested in you – then watch the shift in attitude from the people that previously weren't on board ("Oh, I always loved that actor!!"). Be your own best friend and advise yourself on paper (or your laptop). Whatever negative concoction you are brewing up in your head, it all just seems less frightening when you write it down.

The Tangled Web of Self-Medication

Drugs and alcohol are infamously abused in the entertainment industry and it's not hard to figure out why. When you're feeling insecure, vulnerable and incomplete, self-medication can seem like a respite. But we all know that these crutches have an extremely short shelf life. Irreparably hurting your body in order to feel better in the moment will just bring more hurt into your life – not less. Like attracts like. Sure, alcohol can certainly make you feel sedated and there is a (controversial) school of thought that says small amounts are good for your heart. But I think we're all aware that just because it's a legal substance doesn't mean you can indulge without consequence. Alcohol in excess may put you to sleep but it disrupts your REM cycle, meaning you don't get anything resembling a deep and restful sleep. Besides depleting vitamins from your body, alcohol interferes with your oxygen intake. This in turn can make you more prone to stress, anxiety and depression. A hangover is your body's way of screaming at you that it's in a toxic, acidic state. Did you ever look in the mirror after a night of "overindulgence"? That puffy, bloated frog looking back at you isn't going to be on any casting director's wish list! Listen to your body! Long term abuse of alcohol will damage every organ and system that you have. It can cause cardiovascular disease, liver disease, pancreatitis, damage to your nervous system and cancer. My Dad was a lifelong actor and alcoholic who died of a related cancer at the age of 52. Not a very long life. I could go on and list every recreational drug and its probable consequences, but I think you get my point. The subject of using harmful substances to quiet ones emotional issues is way too complex for me to tackle...all I know is that every day brings with it the possibility to be more evolved, peaceful and whole. You can feel at home with yourself without burning down the house.

There are other, safer ways to quell fear and anxiety. I don't advocate taking medication - either pharmaceutical or alternative – as the first resort in solving emotional issues. But if ingesting pills and whatnot is your preference, then Alternative Medicine is rife with herbs, tinctures, homeopathic and flower remedies. BUT DON'T TAKE THIS AS MEDICAL ADVICE, I'M NOT A DOCTOR! I'll give you the Disclaimer one more time in case you missed it at the top of the book:

All health-related information presented within this book is informational only and should not be considered as a substitute for consultation with a duly-licensed medical doctor. Any attempt to diagnose or treat an illness, minor or major, should come under the direction of a physician or other licensed health care provider. The author is not a medical doctor and does not purport to offer medical advice, make diagnoses or prescribe remedies for specific conditions. Reliance on any health information in this book is solely at your own risk. The author assumes no liability or responsibility for any damage or injury that may occur in any capacity from the use or interpretation of any information in this book.

So! Always ask your doctor if it's safe for you to take specific supplements. In my opinion, a doctor that's either holistically inclined or open to the possibilities of alternative treatments is more the way to go. There are unfortunately a few traditional western MD's out there who haven't learned anything new since they went to medical school many decades ago. There are also a few out there that will blindly dismiss anything not officially approved by the AMA - whether the reason for this is because they have genuine concerns about something that has not gone through their standardized clinical trials, are putting their financial interests first or are simply avoiding any potential lawsuits depends on the doctor in question.

HOWEVER, do not believe that everyone in the alternative medicine world should be unquestionably trusted either. As with western MD's (and every other profession for that matter), there are the dedicated, honest ones and the ones that should be ashamed of themselves. Alternative medicine has become extremely popular in the past few years. While it's beyond great that we've opened our minds to a world of knowledge that is incredibly beneficial, here comes the downside. Everything that's good in this world runs the risk of getting co-opted. So in some cases, Alternative Medicine = Popular = Big Business.

I will state a thousand times that you never should take any supplement, be it herbal or not, without consulting your (open minded!) doctor first because any supplement can be potentially harmful or interfere with medications you may be taking. Just because it's "natural" doesn't mean it's necessarily safe for your unique self and situation. Herbs, vitamins and other forms of supplements are what many prescribed medications are derived from, so *don't* think that you can safely take them without any guidance. Never take any herbal sedatives while you're taking prescription sedatives or anti-depressants. If you want to get off the prescription drug merry-go-round, you'll probably have to follow a protocol and do it gradually – the last thing you want to do is harm yourself in the pursuit of trying to help yourself!

Do your research before blindly reaching for pharmaceutical medication for anxiety and stress. Drugs such as Valium, Halcion, Xanax, etc. are not only addictive, but your body eventually builds up a tolerance to them so that you may need a higher and higher dose to get the same effect. Then there's a little something called Rebound Anxiety, where the drug causes the very symptom that it's supposed to ease. Fun! It has also been recorded year after year that the adverse effects from prescription medicine far outweighs the small numbers for herbal remedies. Please don't trust my say so - do the research!

Supplements

When you have your hopefully progressive and open-minded MD's OK, there are a few different things that may work well to take the edge off your nervousness:

1- Herbs

There are many herbs for relaxation that you can try singularly or in combination with your doctor's OK. The following can be used in the form of tea, tinctures or capsules. You and the Doc will determine which combination and brand works best for you, as your body is unique!

Chamomile is famous for being a mild sedative. People have been using it for years to relax and calm themselves. Chamomile is also good for digestion (it relaxes the gastrointestinal system) and has anti-inflammatory and antibacterial properties.

Valerian has been used for centuries to calm the mind and to ease muscle spasms and cramps. It's primarily used for anxiety, nervousness, panic attacks and insomnia. It won't make you sleepy, it just relaxes you. In case you were wondering, there is no relationship between Valerian and Valium.

Passion Flower is another calming herb that will relax but won't sedate you. Passion Flower's safety as an anti-stress herb has been studied extensively in Europe. It also helps with the craving for and withdrawal from addictive substances like nicotine and alcohol.

Catnip is a member of the mint family. It not only helps relax you in a similar way to Valerian, but it's also used to relieve respiratory infections. So if you have Bronchitis and are going in for an audition, this may give you more bang for your buck! Hey, why are you even getting out of bed if you have Bronchitis?

Hops is not only a flavoring and stability agent in beer - it's also used in herbal medicine as a treatment for nervousness and anxiety. So skip the bloaty beer-face and go straight for the Hops instead (with your MD's approval)!

Kava Kava comes from an ancient plant from the Western Pacific. It's been used specifically for anxiety for hundreds of years by the Polynesians and has been studied for decades in Europe and the US. There has been concern over Kava Kava causing liver toxicity because some manufacturers are using the stems and leaves of the plant, but the traditional method has always been to just use the root. Only buy a brand that solely uses the root, but know that heavy and long term use has been found to elevate liver enzymes. So I would not to take this (without consulting my open-minded doctor!) if I had any liver issues or was a heavy drinker. This herb can work wonders for anxiety, as the effect of a modest amount has been compared to alcohol without the incoherence. Small amounts can improve memory and concentration, but large amounts can cause intoxication to the point of seeming drunk. No - that's not fun, that's just scary. A few people report mild nausea from this herb, but it's actually just the numbing effect that it can have on the stomach.

Skullcap is another herb that should be used with caution because of possible liver toxicity. Although it's suspected that the problems are because another herb, Germander, is sometimes substituted for Scullcap, it's best to be careful if you have existing liver issues. This Native American herb has historically been used for nervousness, depression and anxiety and is now also being used to treat A.D.D. - but PREGNANT WOMEN BEWARE! This herb can induce a miscarriage, so stay the hell away from it!

As you can clearly see, you can never assume that because it's "natural" or simply an herb that it can't hurt you. Although Passionflower has been used safely for many years by many people, in a small few it may cause nausea, drowsiness, vomiting and rapid heartbeat. That sounds like a drug disclaimer -- because it basically is! Many pharmaceuticals are derived from plants and other natural substances. See which combination and brand works best for you, as everyone has their own biochemical individuality. Again, never mix prescription drugs with herbal medicine without supervision from a professional health care provider.

2- Homeopathy

Homeopathy is another way to go. This healing modality uses highly diluted, infinitesimal doses of plant, animal or mineral ingredients to stimulate your body's own immune system and defenses to heal a wide range of physical/emotional issues. In fact, these remedies are diluted to the point where, after 12C, there's nothing left of the original substance. We're talking vibrational essence here, and anyone that's rolling their eyes right now has never tried a homeopathic remedy! The higher the number, the more it's been diluted and therefore the stronger it is. It may be very hard for those of us raised solely on Western Medicine to wrap our minds around how this could ever be effective. There are people that think this is quackery, but there were also those who scoffed at Doctors washing their hands before surgery, so I'll just take a pass on the cynicism! Homeopathy works on the principle that "like cures like" - meaning that the very substance which causes an ailment can, in this much diluted form, teach your body to cure that very same ailment. It has been used for over 200 years in the UK and its origins go back to ancient Greece. According to "Dantas F, Rampes H. Do homeopathic medicines provoke adverse effects? A systematic review. Br Hom J 2000;89,p.35-8", they are non-toxic, non-addictive and very safe. I myself have had great success using homeopathic remedies, as have countless friends of mine. A homeopathic physician is invaluable in helping to discern which of the remedies, at which strength, might be best for you. If you decide that you want to give this a try, see if there's a qualified homeopathic physician in your area or at the very least read up on it thoroughly.

Perhaps the remedy that will be prescribed for you is Gelsemium Sempervirens - this is specifically for stage fright and nervous anticipation! Woo-hoo! Some people have success with Argentum Nitricum, another remedy targeted for anxiety before any kind of performance. The 30C strength, five pellets dissolved under your tongue twice a day for no more than seven days should suffice for most people but everyone's biochemistry is different.

Don't have anything to eat or drink for at least 20 minutes before or 20 minutes after you take homeopathics. There are different schools of thought as to whether or not mint and other aromatics like cinnamon will totally nullify the effects of homeopathic medication. If you're investing the time and effort to take this route, you may want to go all the way and buy mint-free toothpaste made especially for this purpose at any good Health Food store. If you are a gum fanatic, temporarily switch to the fruit flavored variety. Just don't eat anything with mint or cinnamon on the days that you're taking homeopathics. This may be totally unnecessary, but many people purport that it won't work otherwise.

3- Bach Flower Remedies

Bach Flower Remedies work in a similar way to homeopathic medicine. They are safe for anyone, even pregnant women and the elderly, according to all sources. Edward Bach was a British physician who saw all disease as a manifestation of negative emotions. He studied 38 different flowers and plants that he believed cured negative emotions such as fear, anxiety and depression. These remedies are wild flowers steeped in spring water, preserved with 27% grape brandy (hmmmm....maybe that's why you feel better!). Seriously, you're ingesting such a small amount in one dose that the alcohol content wouldn't make a mouse high. I know people who give Bach Flower drops to their dogs to calm them down and swear it's effective, so obviously the placebo effect isn't at work here.

The Bottom Line

Ultimately, you are the sole creator of the demons in your head. Your perception of the events in your life is EVERYTHING. You can choose to see the audition as a place where you're being judged, exposed and humiliated or you can choose to see the audition as a place where you are sharing your unique talent with the world, doing what you love and living your dream. It truly is up to you.

CHAPTER 5:

DISAPPOINTMENT (YOU CAN'T STOP THE WAVES, BUT YOU CAN LEARN TO SURF)

D isappointment - this is such a common challenge that I gave it a chapter of its own. Everyone on the Planet experiences it at one time or another, but it may be one of the most familiar words in an actor's vocabulary. This one emotional response can cause many anguished days and many unhappy lives. No one can hand you a magic formula that ensures you'll never feel disappointment again, but you can definitely gain some measure of control over it.

As with all negative feelings, I think it's important not to deny it – what's the point of burying something that's very real and present? The goal is to feel it and get over it as soon as possible! Feel it - if you need to cry, curse and throw something (preferably soft) then do it - but then you MUST take the next step...

Change Your Perspective! As I stated above, I believe that perception is EVERYTHING. There's a famous Kurosawa film from the 50's called "Rashomon" about a single incident told from different points of view. Each time the vantage point changes, it's an entirely different story. The way you interpret something is simply the product of your very subjective and learned belief system, but it's not Empirical Truth. You can and should change your perspective if it no longer helps you!

Many of you are disheartened - you know that you're a good actor, you know that you're worthy - but not getting a job can make you doubt the entire business and maybe even yourself. You feel that you gave a great audition but they "rejected" you. You can't help but take this personally because it's your voice, your physicality, your creativity that's being rebuffed. Well, that's one perspective, but if you're truly performing at the top of your game, then I can offer you another. Producers and directors are waiting to fall in love in the room. Just because they aren't in love with you for this role doesn't necessarily mean that they don't think you're great or you won't be "the one" for something else. A fabulous comedian, Deon Cole, gave me an analogy that I love and will take liberties to paraphrase here. Let's say you have a beige suit and you need to buy beige shoes to go with it. You go out to the store and get a pair that you think will be perfect, but when you get them home and see them with the suit they don't match after all. There are a thousand different shades of beige and until you put the shoes together with the suit, it's impossible to know which will be the right one. So you may say "Hey, I'm perfect for this -- they say they want beige and I'm beige!", but when you go in and audition they're thinking "I need a beige with more yellow - this beige has blue undertones". We don't always know this until you're in the room and we see you read it. This isn't necessarily a reflection of our opinion of your talent. We are likely just looking for a different shade of beige! So there you are - feeling rejected - but we may very well be thinking that you'll be right for something else. There are so many reasons as to why someone gets the job or not, but in the end it's a pretty subjective decision. In the eyes of the particular team that's at the helm, it simply was or wasn't your role. I mentioned this subjective factor earlier - one producer loves you but the other one just doesn't get you - hey, you won't be universally loved no matter how great you are or aren't. That's just life.

So what can you actively do to get out of this depressed mind-set? First of all, any movement is better than no movement. Sitting like a slug and going over your "failure" in your mind only gets my sympathy for 24 hours. Then you must force yourself to move!

~ Go for a walk, go to the gym, the park, the movies, a museum - anyplace where you will encounter people and sights that you wouldn't have experienced if you hadn't ventured out. Who knows what adventures, small or large, will come from this?

~Call and/or get together with a friend who thinks you're enormously talented (or at least someone that believes in you). Be careful not to pick someone that's just as disgruntled as you are to wallow and commiserate with - that's simply two people lying in their own piss by a dumpster. Nice image. A friend will help you to see things more clearly and can provide you with positive reinforcement. A friend knows who you are and all of your wonderful attributes. A friend can remind you of those things even if you've temporarily forgotten them.

~Write in a journal – keep going until you get all of your frustration out and down on the page. Then make an effort to stop and make a switch towards the positive. Write down each and every good thing that you can think of about yourself and your journey. Chart your course as an actor from the very first time you fell in love with it and note how far you've come - from the tiniest accomplishment to the largest. It's important in these moments to remember that you're not running a race with anyone (that includes yourself) and that there's always another audition coming down the road.

Everything, everything, everything (I'll repeat it a million times if you need me to!) is presented to you as a lesson. Everything. Although The Good Times are lots of fun, there are very few major epiphanies or soul-deepening changes that are made when all is well. I didn't say none, I said very few. Much of our growth comes in packages that aren't very pretty. We all know that a caterpillar has to gestate in a gooey cocoon to become a butterfly. As it is in Nature, so it is in our psyche.

So we always should ask ourselves "What's the lesson here?". If you can't come up with an immediate answer, then you have to trust that it will become apparent at the appropriate time. Not when you demand it, but when you can understand and handle it. This holds true for conflicts in our personal lives as well, but we're focusing here on career disappointments. Perhaps the most common one is that the role you desperately wanted went to someone else. There are many possible lessons here as to why this was the case: Maybe there are still some things emotionally that you need to learn. Maybe there are some things spiritually that you need to learn. Maybe there are some crucial nuts and bolts acting or life principals that you think you've mastered but actually haven't. Maybe you were ready but the producer had a specific vision for this part that you simply didn't fit in to (as in the beige suit metaphor above). Maybe you fit very well but so did another actor and their dues-paying-days were now cosmically deemed over (as will yours be one day soon if you're on the right path). There are so many elements that go into these decisions and the Universe doesn't always adhere to your script! The bottom line is that this particular role was never meant to be yours - if it was, you would have gotten it. Harsh? I don't think so, because when you DO get a role, there are scores of other actors out there who desperately wanted it as well. Do you think that your role was probably meant for them? No way - you're thrilled because now it's your turn. This one is yours and it's meant for no one else.

Maybe you're unhappy because even though jobs do come your way, it simply doesn't happen enough. Or maybe you're grateful that you get hired but are dissatisfied because they aren't the kind of roles that you ultimately want.

Okay, so when things don't go your way, what can you learn from this perceived "set back"? Well, that depends on *you* - because even though the dilemma is certainly common, each one of us is on a very unique road.

~ Maybe you need to reevaluate how you're auditioning or fine-tune something in your acting. Do you think you're beyond that? If so, that may very well be the problem right there! Years ago, I was fortunate enough to see Jessica Tandy and Hume Cronyn in "Foxfire" on Broadway and went backstage to meet them. If you don't know who they were, brush up on your Theater History because (although they've passed away) this long-married couple was considered Acting Royalty for a few decades. Ms. Tandy was the original Blanche Dubois opposite Marlon Brando in "Streetcar", but you may remember her as the star of the film "Driving Miss Daisy". In the few minutes I spent with them, it was obvious that she and Mr. Cronyn were still very much in love after 41 years - they were married for 52 years until her death. I was struck by her incredibly youthful and enthusiastic energy, but above all I'll never forget how she responded to my praise of her performance. She said "What I love most about acting is that you always have another chance tomorrow to try and get it right". If this 74 year old actress with three Tony Awards and an Academy Award didn't think that she was beyond discovery about her craft, then neither should you!!! Get over your ego (which is really just a mask for your insecurity) and have the courage to reassess yourself. You'll no doubt discover things that will reinvigorate you, because show me someone that thinks they know everything and I'll show you someone that's probably in a bit of a rut.

~ Maybe you have a few unhealthy perceptions and learned behaviors that need to be addressed before you could gracefully handle the demands that this job would have presented you. Yes, of course there are successful actors out there that behave badly and some big stars that are screwed up - but that's nothing to aspire to. If you're thinking "I'll take that!", then you've got a lot to learn. If you have success without any semblance of inner peace and grati-tude, that's simply a different kind of misery. Being successful will make you happy initially, but if you were emotionally challenged beforehand - watch out. When the dust settles after the initial rush of "Wooo-hoo I'm rich and famous", you're inevitably confronted with the Same Old Miserable You and it can be devastating. Before, at least you could attribute your unhappiness to a lack of success. Now there's nothing left to blame but the mirror. Some people choose instead to lash out at those around them and very quickly get a bad reputation. Show me someone that's inconsiderate or unpleasant to be around and I'll show you an unhappy person. On top of it all, many people will cheer when "the schmuck" loses his or her box office appeal and becomes a has-been. Oh, what fun this kind of success is! I truly doubt that this is anyone's idea of happiness.

So, if you recognize that you have some unresolved issues that may be getting in your way (and don't they always?), you really need to start healing the wounds now.

It's news to no one that many actors are emotionally vulnerable. This is a business however, and sometimes an actor finds him-or-herself dealing with what can be a cold bureaucracy. Navigating this can be a huge challenge for many of you. Not getting a role that you want can be a blessing (yes, I believe that) if you haven't yet learned how to be a diplomat. Great actors have lost their careers over this, so take it seriously. A very special actor that complains about everything all the time (whether you're right or not doesn't matter) gets branded as trouble. As much as they may love your talent, you're expendable to them. Unless you're already a big star, your work won't speak for itself. Even if you are a big star, no one protects you from the media anymore and the crap you say at 2:30AM is all over the internet by 2:32AM. You must learn to be gracious to everyone. Am I saying to be a doormat? Not at all. I'm saying that you are there as the friendly, cooperative actor and your agent or manager can act as "the bad guy"! That is part of their function (sorry, all my agent and manager friends). Whatever it is, take a few deep breaths and do your best to put on your game-face until you can call your manager or agent. Don't make a scene, don't hold up production - this will just come back to haunt you, no matter how right you are! If it's something trivial but annoying, don't make any bitchy comments on the set - just suck it up and then go home to your loved ones and complain to them. I'm sure there are people who would scoff at this advice, but over the decades I've seen how destructive this behavior can be to an actor's career. You hopefully won't get a big job until you've learned the importance of getting along with everyone (or at least how to pretend)!

There are many actors that are self-involved and I totally understand why that is. An actor can spend many years being subservient to the industry, metaphorically naked, putting him or herself out there just to be "rejected" many times over. So I can see how someone who is being judged daily on their physical features, their emotional life and their imagination can become fixated on those very things. In a business where promotion plays a huge part in success, can we blame an actor for beating their own drum if self-promotion is the only means available to them? If you don't have a strong agent or a great manager, it can seem like the only person that's truly looking out for you is you. So I can sympathize with this.

But there are those of you (not many in my experience, I'm happy to say) that are so self-involved that you can't see beyond your own needs. My dime store psychology says that anyone with absolutely no regard for others has some serious self-worth issues. When you're so desperate for recognition and success that you aren't pleasant to be around (at best) or destructive to others (at worst), you are never, never, never going to be happy. Everyone knows at least one person like this (I hope it's not you, but if it is, I still love you - get help!).

I wish that the following story was an isolated incident, but unfortunately it's not. An actress told me that she was once in a waiting room for a cold audition with a few other women. There were three scenes out on the table and they all began studying them. Within moments an actress came out of the audition room and gave the others the heads up that they were only doing scene three, and not to even bother with the other two. The women were all grateful and just concentrated on scene three. When my actress friend went into the audition - you guessed it - scene three was the only one that they weren't doing. So this actress was so insecure about herself that she felt she had to undermine her fellow actresses to get the edge. I've heard variations of this same kind of story many times over the years. There's a deep-seated fear in these actors that goes beyond the financial and career considerations regarding whether or not you get the job. The real fear is that *you may not be good enough* to get the job on your own merit. Getting the job, fairly or not, becomes so twisted up with a lack of self-worth that you're willing to ignore whatever integrity you have. The fear of disappointment in yourself if you don't make it says that "only something external can make me happy because I'm unworthy of happiness as I am". It screams "I'm not enough".

So now you've ensured that even if you get the job, you'll ultimately be unhappy anyway - because you still haven't addressed that gnawing feeling that "I'm not enough". Don't kid yourself – it doesn't go away with the outside validation of a job alone. If you yourself don't believe it, you'll now just live in fear that your "lack" will be exposed one day. Believe me, I've known a Star or two like this. I want to be clear - this is NOT to be confused with the occasional common introspection of "am I really good enough?" that most actors share. I'm talking about the person that takes this to a destructive level.

If you're experiencing feelings of jealousy (fear) or discontent (fear), you may want to try taking small steps towards the Abundance Theory. This is the concept that there's always enough happiness in the world for everyone, so there's no reason to think that someone else's fortune somehow subtracts from your own. Most of us have felt competitive or territorial at one time or another. Sometimes it can seem benign compared to the "sabotaging actress" example above, but if these thoughts are left unchecked they can easily slide into an unworthy place. This includes everything from the guy that really wants his friends to do well - as long as he's gotten his own success first – to the actress that says mean things about a competing actress' nose job. When you do this, you're saying that there's not enough opportunity and love in the world to go around so I can't afford to be generous. OUCH!! Someone needs a huge mind-shift! If you think that there's not enough, there won't be. The Universe simply mirrors how you're thinking and feeling – in this case "there's not enough" – and magnifies that back to you.

> *What we see depends mainly*
> *on what we look for.*
> *- Sir John Lubbock*

When you're jealous and bitter, the Universe receives your message and gives you more things to be jealous and bitter about. You then see these crappy results as proof of your theory that the world sucks. As this cycle repeats over and over, disappointment eventually hardens your heart. You may say "Hey, I started out believing but it was life that knocked it out of me". I say that you may want to rethink your concept of "believing" and "expectation". You may have expected circumstances to go a certain way, but when the Universe had a different path in mind, you saw that as some sort of cosmic betrayal. If I've learned anything, it's that expectations can be a bitch. If you aren't willing to release them, you will probably miss out on many of life's best and unexpected journeys. If expectations aren't met, many people assume defeat and – consciously or unconsciously - stop their own careers cold. However, when you believe in something, it takes a hell of a lot more than disappointment to knock it out of you. Stephen King's first novel "Carrie" was rejected 30 times. There are scores of famous artists out there that would have simply died on the vine had they let the defeat of their original expectations crush them. The ones that make it all the way through usually have a tenacious belief in their own talent and don't let crippling jealousy or perceived setbacks stop them.

So if you see yourself anywhere in this chapter, try something different. Try to not measure the amount or size of your roles against anyone or anything else. Make an effort to actually be happy for another actor when they get a job. Respond to their achievement today in the same positive way that you'd like them to respond to yours tomorrow. Is it possible that some of this good energy that's now flowing out will actually be acknowledged by the Universe and come back to you? Have you been reading this book?!

Sit down and make a list of everything you're grateful for – I know that this simple act seems elementary and naïve but you've got to start the healing somewhere. Don't get me wrong – I don't have the recipe for How To Make Everything Go Your Way. No matter who you are or what you do, nothing can - or even should - ensure that.

Whenever something messes up your plan or goal, consider that maybe the Universe has a better idea and don't be so quick to judge it negatively. It's very possible that what you desperately want today may not really be the best circumstance for you. Be willing to let go of your expectations and allow something else that's wonderful in. Remember that things have a tendency to work out exactly the way they're supposed to. Ask yourself how the perceived "bad" events that you're presented with can make you stronger and wiser. If you can do this, then everything that happens can be seen as your progression towards a happier and more peaceful existence.

Give me one good reason not to shift your perspective and reflect on what's presently beautiful and good in your life right now? All of these things are there – if you can't see them, it's because you're too busy making goo-goo eyes at some intangible deity to really look. Waiting for some magical, external thing to make you whole and happy is denying the joy that's right in front of you. That's just Crazy-Town. There's a reason why Beckett's "Waiting For Godot" is such a classic!

I'll end this chapter with some mind-blowing wisdom from one of the great poets, Edna St. Vincent Millay. This is from "Renascence", which nudged me off my Pity Pot many years ago and introduced me to the concept that your happiness is solely up to you:

The world stands out on either side
No wider than the heart is wide;
Above the world is stretched the sky,
No higher than the soul is high.
The heart can push the sea and land
Farther away on either hand;
The soul can split the sky in two,
And let the face of God shine through.
But East and West will pinch the heart
That can not keep them pushed apart;
And he whose soul is flat—the sky
Will cave in on him by and by.

CHAPTER 6:

EVERYTHING IS AN ART (EXPRESSING YOURSELF IN EVERYDAY LIFE)

This is a tiny last chapter, but it was too important for me to leave out. One of the great things about being an actor is that everything that happens in your life can help to serve your craft. There are those that think about acting 24/7. There are actors who think of it simply as a job and leave it all behind when they go home. Although actors have many different ways of approaching their profession, most would agree that their personal life experience is essential to the process. There are many ways to accumulate this personal store of knowledge, and many types of knowledge to seek out.

Seeing The Pattern

Everything in our world is connected. The veins in a leaf are very much like the veins in our bodies. Reflexology teaches us that points in our feet and hands correspond to all of our organs. Iridology tells us that the map that is in our eyes can show us the health of our system, glands and organs more accurately than many traditional tests. The eco-system of the earth is very similar to the eco-system in our intestines (yes, there's an entire world living in there!). Every living being with a consciousness is connected, as we are all part of a gigantic tapestry. So there's an awful lot to learn from seemingly unconnected things, because ultimately everything is linked in one way or another.

One of the reasons that sports are so popular is because they are perfect metaphors for our daily "trials and tribulations". So much of life is about achievement, competition, teamwork, the transient nature of winning and the invaluable lessons of losing. Sports can teach you incredible life lessons in a way that's understandable and relevant. Any parent knows the value of this in regards to their kids, but it definitely goes beyond the Little League Team. There's a wonderful book called "Golf Is Not a Game of Perfect" by Bob Rotella that is every bit as instructional for your life as it is for your Golf game. There are many correlations between how to approach the ball and how to approach an audition: the complete preparation, the absolute focus, imagining your goal and perfecting your individual style. You can learn how to accept "victory or defeat" graciously and understand how you may have gotten in your own way so that tomorrow you can go out there and do better. Bobby Jones, a very famous Amateur Golfer, has one of the greatest quotes. Applicable to most everything in life including acting, he said "Competitive golf is played mainly on a five-and-a-half-inch course...the space between your ears."

You can substitute baseball or basketball for golf – really, just about any sport has relatable metaphors for life issues. Chess is classically used in the Arts as a metaphor for the psychological war between two characters, but it can also help us to sharpen our life skills. It can teach you the value of considering the consequences before you make any move. Also, you can't move the Rook in the same way that you do the Knight - just as you can't expect Person A in your life to behave like Person B. We can throw these metaphors around all day, but you get the point. Absolutely everything is connected and therefore, if we choose to, we can learn from it all.

Art and Perception

What's your definition of being an "Artist"? The word conjures up many images, some of which can be construed in the negative as pretentious or elitist. Some people feel that you can't call yourself an Artist if you're not actively producing any tangible "Art". I think it's important to open up this concept and put some of the same care, thought, inspiration and heart into everything we do on a daily basis. If you're presently in a "survival job" and feel that your creativity can only be nurtured when you're acting, you might want to take another look at that limiting belief. One of the Dictionary definitions of the word Artist is simply "a person whose work exhibits exceptional skill". It stands to reason then, that whatever you're doing at the moment can be considered an Art. You just need to stop thinking that it has no relevance to what you really want to be doing. One of the most important skills you want to hone as an actor is your ability to relate and communicate. Can you honestly say that you can't work on those skills in ANY situation you find yourself in that involves other people? Most jobs require at least some interaction with others, and right there you have an opportunity to grow. To a large extent, I believe that an actor is only as good as the choices that he or she makes within a scene. Every choice you make as an actor essentially comes from your life experience - the scenarios you've witnessed, the scenarios you've participated in, the people you've interacted with. Being in an environment outside of the acting world provides the perfect opportunity to add some different angles, characters and colors to your palette.

So - if you're experiencing a somewhat negative attitude about having to be a Waiter, Bartender, Personal Trainer or Temp, see if you can reexamine that. Think about how you can turn the challenge of this survival-job time into a creative gymnasium that will work for instead of against you.

If you find yourself having to get work as a Waiter or Waitress, how can you be the absolute best at it? What can you do to make your customers have a better experience? You can use your unique personality to your advantage here. I eat in restaurants 90% of the time (hey, I'm busy!) and I've been known to bring in the waiter or waitress that I met at dinner the other night for a role that I'm working on today. These particular individuals weren't necessarily gorgeous - more times than not it was their personality that attracted me. Can you pride yourself in not just reciting The Specials of the Day, but presenting them in such a way that they sound enticing? Finding just the right subtle approach that will make the customer feel like you're their friend is a great step towards knowing how to walk into an audition. Exploit your skills - if you've got a steel-trap memory and can take 4 orders without writing them down, do so (I'm impressed!). If you're Mr. or Ms. Funny, wriggle your sense of humor into your customer's dining experience. Good practice for putting a bit of comedy into a drama! Waiters and waitresses sometimes have to deal with rude people who see them basically as servants. That sounds like great training in How to Finesse a Rude Agent or a Dismissive Director! Vow to be the best and make waiting tables an Art.

If you're Bartending, there are infinite possibilities for this, depending on what type of place you're working at. Make yourself the reason people come in – become a Mixologist and create new drinks that can't be gotten elsewhere. Your personality and imagination can be used to create a persona that helps to shape the ambience of the place you're working (unless it's a strip club – then you're on your own!). This is an important job, because the tone of an establishment (friendly, fun, sophisticated, trendy or laid back) can be influenced by the Bartender. Because you may be dealing with inebriated people whose social etiquette has vaporized, there will probably be a few altercations and interesting exchanges on a nightly basis. Use them as a powerful opportunity to observe human behavior and to sharpen your communication skills: listening, understanding different points of view, how to get through to someone that isn't listening, all with a focused and cool head. There's great value in knowing which battles are worth fighting and which aren't. Being that you'll be sober and they might not be, it's also an opportunity to see what you look like when you've had too much to drink. Any service industry job can be a great learning experience and yes, definitely an Art if you do it the right way.

I could go on and list examples for every conceivable survival job that an actor might have, but the basic principles are the same. These jobs allow you to observe life and interact with people in all their quirky wonder. The things you experience in these jobs today can be accessed and used in your acting tomorrow.

Virtually anything that's executed with intelligence, creativity, ethics, care and love can be considered an Art.

"If a man is called a streetsweeper, he should sweep streets even as Michelangelo painted, or Beethoven composed music, or Shakespeare wrote poetry...."
- Martin Luther King, Jr.

SUMMING IT ALL UP

When you perceive this business as one big adventure, you are freed from the tyranny of your own expectations. Be grateful for your achievements so far and have an open heart to whatever the Universe has in store for you. It's self-defeating to have a limited appreciation for your present accomplishments because your eye is always on a bigger, shinier prize. I have known many actors over the years with a resume that 90% of actors would be envious of who have totally forgotten that they were once in that 90%. Their definition of success keeps getting redefined, the line in the sand erased and moved, as each accomplishment becomes almost inconsequential in the face of that next thing that they don't yet have. Where does it end - is there such a thing as an apex of achievement? Even if there was, what then? You're left with yourself, that's what – and it's the same self that you started out with. You intrinsically know that all of the outside validation in the world means nothing if you yourself don't feel worthy.

> *"A man cannot be comfortable*
> *without his own approval."*
> *- Ralph Waldo Emerson*

I'm neither your Therapist nor your Mother, although I'm probably repeating myself as many times as they do: it doesn't take a rocket scientist to know that appreciation and gratitude for what you have here and now can only make you a happier person. If it helps to make it a ritual, every night before you go to sleep you should make that list - short or long - of the things you're grateful for today. Anything at all that's a positive for you - a friendly exchange at the store or a good workout at the gym - counts!

"To know you have enough is to be rich"
                                    - Lao Tsu

Some of the most talented people I know don't get hired nearly enough and some lesser talents never stop working. You may end up leaving this business altogether or you may end up a huge star. The events that happen in your life aren't nearly as important as how you choose to perceive and handle them.

The greatest minds in our recorded history believed this - Shakespeare, Gibran, Tolstoy, Jefferson - why in the world shouldn't you???

*"There is nothing either good or
bad, but thinking makes it so."*
                          - William Shakespeare

*"Your living is determined not so much by
what life brings to you as by the attitude you
bring to life; not so much by what happens to
you as by the way your mind looks
at what happens. "*
                          - Kahlil Gibran

"Happiness does not depend on outward things, but on the way we see them."

- Tolstoy

"Nothing can stop the man with the right mental attitude from achieving his goal; nothing on earth can help the man with the wrong mental attitude."

- Thomas Jefferson

If you can look at yourself honestly and take steps to change what isn't working for you anymore, you're on the right road. When you're on the right road, life will simply unfold in a way that will either be everything you dreamed of or something entirely unpredictable — but one way another, it will be an amazing adventure.

Trust that.

CPSIA information can be obtained
at www.ICGtesting.com
Printed in the USA
LVHW040104301118
598743LV00009B/29/P